SQUIRRELS

BY ?

Keith Laidler

SQUIRRELS

IN BRITAIN

?

DAVID & CHARLES
Newton Abbot London North Pomfret (Vt)

British Library Cataloguing in Publication Data
Laidler, Keith
  Squirrels.
  1. Squirrels — Great Britain — Behaviour
  2. Mammals — Great Britain — Behaviour
  I. Title
  599'.3232   QL737.R68

  ISBN 0-7153-7825-2

Library of Congress Catalog Card Number 80-66421

Typeset by ABM Typographics Limited, Hull
and printed in Great Britain
by Biddles Limited, Guildford
for David & Charles (Publishers) Limited
Brunel House Newton Abbot Devon

Published in the United States of America
by David & Charles Inc
North Pomfret Vermont 05053 USA

Contents

Introduction-the Squirrels
Around Us

If the tree squirrel did not exist, then it would surely have been created by some inventive artist. Where would fairy tales, myths, legends and modern-day children's stories be without that inquisitive and engaging creature? Probably no animal in the world can match it for vivacity and sheer cuteness. Nimble, alert, with big eyes and a long sensuous tail, the squirrel is certainly one of the loveliest of all British mammals. Whether it is the graceful native red squirrel (a subspecies unique to Great Britain) or the introduced American grey, to see a squirrel adds immeasurably to any country walk.

The squirrels of Britain are but a small sample of a rodent group—the sciurids—which contains more than 250 species, living in almost every conceivable terrestrial habitat. Despite the fact that the squirrel is really little more than a tree-living rat with a bushy tail, it has a strangely warming effect on people, espcially the female of our species. Women who scream at the sight of a mouse or rat and shy away from contact with their child's pet hamster, turn misty-eyed and sentimental whenever a squirrel sits on its haunches to eat a nut. There must be something about the squirrel, but exactly what?

In recent years, much new information has been collected on these intriguing tree creatures, providing fascinating insights into their way of life. Their life cycle is now known in great detail: what and how they eat, conditions inside their drey 'houses', their noisy mating chases with up to thirty males pursuing and fighting for a single female, parental care, and how the young squirrel develops to adulthood. The adaptations of the squirrel to its 'life-support system'—the tree—

illustrate the remarkable interrelationships of plant and animal communities. It seems amazing that it does not entirely kill off the woodlands on which it feeds—a single squirrel will consume upwards of two million pine seeds each year!

Many cherished beliefs have been demolished as the secrets of the squirrel's way of life have been unravelled. It is not altogether the friendly little creature of most children's stories. While it is a social animal, organised into (male-dominated) hierarchies in which the 'top man' gets the pick of the good things of life, each squirrel lives a rather solitary life, possessing a territory which it will defend fiercely against all comers: fights, bites and chases form a normal part of a typical squirrel's day. Contrary to popular belief, the squirrel does not hibernate: it may stay inside its nest during damp, wet weather, but it can be seen out and about on even the coldest days. Nor does the creature possess the ability to think ahead to the coming winter—the usual explanations given for its well-known habit of burying nuts underground or in the holes of trees. The animal does benefit from these food caches in winter, but recent experiments have shown that this 'intelligent' behaviour is really no more than the workings of an organic computer, programmed to react predictably to a series of environmental cues. Upset these cues and you can have squirrels 'burying' nuts in solid concrete at the bottom of chair legs (see page 64)! Another current misconception is that the grey squirrel, first known to be introduced into Britain from America in 1876, owes its success to its systematic premeditated murder of our native red squirrel. This is certainly not true. The reasons for the meteoric rise of the grey squirrel are many and varied, but the concurrent decline of the red is due as much to man's tampering with the environment as to the grey squirrel's sciuricidal tendencies.

Squirrels are absorbing to watch—if you know how to find them. Suburban squirrels are easy; some even advertise their presence by entering houses to 'beg' for titbits. But squirrels in the country, especially the native red, are much more difficult to locate and observe. This book shows the novice where to look and, more importantly, what to look for. The tracks and signs of the squirrel are quite distinctive, and with a little intelligent application it should be possible to discover just where in your area the squirrels have their homes, and to which species they belong. The little-known squirrel marking-sites— the woodland 'notice boards' where each animal leaves its own personal calling card—are described in detail. Once located, we can observe the squirrels without modifying their natural behaviour, photograph them, and even eavesdrop on squirrel-to-squirrel conversations by translating the many postural and tail movements that go to make up squirrel sign-language.

Pretty as they are, in many parts of the world squirrels are a pest. Several industries find them more than just a nuisance, especially forestry. Where squirrels are around in small numbers, the damage— mainly bark-stripping—is minimal, but, with high populations they do so much harm that whole plantations can become uneconomic. In certain parts of the United Kingdom the grey squirrel's attacks on trees have already reached critical proportions, and it is controlled (though seldom with 100 per cent success) by trapping, poisoning and shooting. Instead of employing these inefficient, expensive methods of reducing the squirrel population, it will be argued that there is a very good case for attempting some form of biological control. Reintroducing the pine marten, and perhaps the wild cat, both of which were once native to most of the British Isles, would be an inexpensive and efficient ecological solution to the squirrel problem. Strange as it may seem, a squirrel 'birth pill' would also prove extremely effective and easy to administer.

This is not to say that we should rid these islands completely of these bushy-tailed rodents. Even if it were possible, few of us would consider total extermination desirable. In fact, in several parts of the country, for example in some Forestry Commission plantations, the red squirrel is actively encouraged. And it is possible to aid our own unique sub-species of red squirrel while at the same time keeping the grey invader in check. It is hoped that everyone who reads this book will be able to help one of the most beautiful of our native fauna to remain bright-eyed and bushy-tailed.

1
Rodents in General and Squirrels in Particular

Squirrels belong to the most successful of all mammal groups, the Order Rodentia. Squirrels apart, the world teems with rodents: guinea pig, chinchilla, beaver, coypu and the ubiquitous rat and mouse are all members of this most international of animal forms. Of the sixteen Orders of living mammals, the rodents have by far the greatest number of recognised species, living in almost every imaginable terrestrial niche. To date, nearly 3,000 are known, far in excess of the puny 200 or so species of primates, the Order to which man, the so-called Lord of Creation, belongs.

The rodents also have an infinitely longer and far more respectable pedigree than most mammals. Their origin begins far back in geological time, approximately 54 million years ago, during the late Palaeocene. This is very early in the history of the mammals. If we were to reduce the time that life has existed on earth until the present day to a single, twenty-four hour day, the mammals appear at 22.48 and 55 seconds and the rodents soon after at 23.32 and 40 seconds. Modern man is very much the late comer—he arrives on the scene at 15 seconds to midnight!

Prior to the rodents, fossil records reveal the existence of super-ficially rat-like forms, the Multituberculates. Named for the numerous cusps (or tubercles) on their molar teeth, these creatures flourished throughout the Mesozoic, holding sway for an astonishing 100 million years. Then suddenly they were no more, having been eliminated in competition with the newly evolved and far more efficient rodents, who took their place and have held it to the present day. The earliest fossil rodents are from North America. They are of the family Paramyidae and they already show all the diagnostic features of their Order. The anatomy of these ancestral rodents was that of a generalised scampering mammal, very like the rat (*Rattus* spp) in its method of locomotion. A few million years later, there was an astonishing 'explosion' of the rodents into many different forms. Diversification of shape, size and anatomy proceeded very rapidly during the next 20 million years or so, new families of rodent evolved and new habitats were invaded and conquered. Although the fossil evidence is sparse, there must have been a continuing adaptive radiation of these forms, for the majority of living families of rodents had appeared by the end of the Oligocene (approximately 26 million years ago). The family Sciuridae appeared during this epoch, evolving gradually towards the presentday stock of marmots, chipmunks and tree squirrels. The remaining families all came into existence during the following geological period (except the Muridae, the family to which both rats and mice belong, which did not appear until the early Pliocene, 7 million years ago).

Like most other rodents, squirrels are small and because of this their remains were often overlooked by early fossil hunters. This led to the erroneous belief that squirrels and other rodents formed a very small proportion of the vertebrate population. However, modern intensive exploration has resulted in the recovery of many more small mammal fossils, proving that rodents, including squirrels, were an abundant segment of the ancient fauna (fig 1). Because of this development, and the rather large number of fossils now available, rodent remains are invaluable in the separation of successive geological horizons, a vital aid to accurate dating of finds.

The Power-shears of the Animal Kingdom

The effect the rodents' gnawing way of life has had on their jaw muscles, or on the modification of jaw and skull to accommodate these muscles, has been used by Palaeontologists to help distinguish the main 'blood-related' clans among the Rodentia.

Although primitive in general appearance, the rodents have been responsible for one big innovation in the basic mammalian blueprint: they possess by far the most efficient gnawing equipment of any mammal, indeed of any vertebrate. The Order's title, Rodentia, derives from the Latin *rodere*, to gnaw, and the rodents are the power-shears of the animal kingdom, forever carving, cutting and snipping their way through a multitude of different materials.

In even the earliest rodents, and in all modern forms, there has been extensive modification of dental equipment. Most primates possess two incisor teeth, one canine, two premolar and three molar teeth *on each side* of both their upper and lower jaw. The biologist describes this arrangement in the 'dental formula' $\frac{2}{2} \frac{1}{1} \frac{2}{2} \frac{3}{3}$, the digits above the lines describing the teeth of one side of the upper jaw, and those below describing the teeth in the lower jaw. As you can see, the different teeth of both upper and lower jaws are equal, and form 'pairs'; there are for example two incisor pairs and one canine pair. By contrast, squirrels and all other rodents have only a single pair of incisors, no canines, a variable number of premolars (usually one pair) and three molar pairs.

The molars and premolars are very similar in the Rodentia and both show modifications for grinding, a reflection of most rodents' dependence on vegetable matter for sustenance. The single incisor pair bears the brunt of all direct gnawing. In the face of such erosive pressure, the teeth of most other animals, including ourselves and even the dentally well-endowed dog, would rapidly wear away. The rodents have overcome this problem by evolving teeth which grow throughout their life. Only the anterior 30-60 per cent of tooth surface is covered by enamel and growth rates vary from between 2 and 5mm per year, the highest rates being found in those species which spend the greatest time with their teeth to the grindstone. In the tree squirrels the rate of incisor growth is 2-3mm per year, a figure which reflects the intermediate hardness of their staple diet—nuts and seeds.

This arrangement is fine provided the upper and lower incisors meet and wear down at the same rate. When they don't, the animal can be in serious trouble. On rare occasions, because of deformity or breakage of these chisel-teeth, the incisor pair is thrown out of alignment. When this happens the teeth continue to grow indefinitely and may become a positive threat to the owner. The lower incisors are no problem; simply growing forward and upward in a wide arc which, while perhaps looking unsightly and being unwieldy in enclosed situations, is not as serious as the uncontrolled growth of the upper incisors. These often spiral tightly, curving inexorably around and up, growing first through the throat and eventually through the snout, locking the jaws closed and, in most cases, resulting in the animal dying a lingering death from starvation.

Such a unique set of teeth obviously requires adaptations of anatomy and musculature to work efficiently. As might be expected in such resourceful creatures, the Order Rodentia is not found wanting when it comes to adaptations. In all other mammals there are projections on a socket-shaped depression in the skull which prevent the backward and forward motion of the lower jaw. The rodents lack these bony protrusions, and their jaws can consequently slide either to the front or to the rear. Such 'dislocation' of the jaw is no mere party trick: it is a very useful arrangement, giving the rodents, in effect, a two-geared dual-purpose dentition. When forward gear is engaged the lower jaw advances, the upper and lower molars are separated from one another, and the upper and lower incisors come together for gnawing. In reverse gear the jaw slides back, the incisors disengage and the molars meet for chewing. These jaw movements are brought about by the action of three muscles: the temporal, pterygoid, and especially the masseter. It is the evolutionary changes in the length and position of the masseter that have brought about the three main categories of rodent jaw, anatomy, one of which is the squirrel-like or sciuromorphous arrangement.

The World's Squirrels

With the help of this musculature and their unique set of shears, the rodents have spread throughout the world. The Order is so huge that it is divided into four sub-orders of which only one, the Sciuromorpha or squirrel-like rodents, concerns us here. The remaining sub-orders are the Myomorpha, a world-wide group which includes rats, mice and their kin; the Caviomorpha (chinchillas, agoutis and guinea pigs), whose

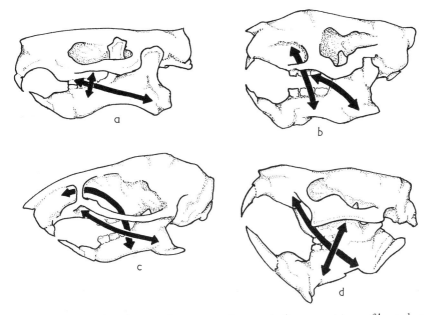

1. Skulls of the four basic rodent types. Arrows indicate positions of branches of the masseter muscle. (a) Protrogomorphous type (b) Hystricomorphous type (c) Myomorphous type (d) Sciuromorphous type—the squirrel-type rodents.

range encompasses most of the Americas; and the Phiomorpha of Africa. As the Sciuromorpha includes more than 1,300 named forms, it is more than enough to be going on with! Fortunately, the squirrel-like rodents are further subdivided into various super-families. One of these, the Sciuroidea, contains the true squirrels, family Sciuridae. Even here there are more than 40 genera and over 250 species to contend with.

The true squirrels are a cosmopolitan group, living in all the continents except Australia (where, apart from bats, there are no indigenous placental mammals), various islands and the extreme polar regions. Within this extensive range they inhabit many different ecological communities. They are found in desert, prairie, tundra and the high mountains. Some live all their lives in the tree canopy, while others (the burrowing forms) may never climb anything higher than a grass tussock. The ground-living species include squirrels which can remain inactive for more than six months of the year, whereas the tree dwellers never hibernate or aestivate. These latter are probably the most widespread: they inhabit most types of forest, varying from dense tropical rain-forest to the great conifer woodlands of the northern taiga.

Ground squirrels are found between the farthest southern limits of the temperate region and the Arctic Circle. They exist in both the Old and the New Worlds. They are invariably diurnal and are characterised by their habit of living in burrows although some, such as the golden mantled squirrel, *Citellus lateralis*, are said to climb well. Many of the ground squirrels form stable social communities; the prairie dog (*Cynomys* spp) lives in extensive 'cities' many square miles in extent: in 1901, one city was estimated to cover an area 240 miles by 100 miles, and to contain 400 *million* prairie dogs! The burrows are cleverly constructed so that air circulates freely within the tunnel, probably the first mammalian air-conditioning system. Other species, like the thirteen-striped ground squirrel, are not particularly fond of company and never form large social groups.

The habitats of the ground-squirrel species are many and varied. Some, like the marmot, are found in snow-covered mountainous regions such as the European Alps. Others inhabit arid treeless plains, deserts, grasslands or forests. Most ground squirrels are omnivorous: their diet includes seeds, fruits, berries, roots and the succulent shoots of plants, insects, earthworms and even other small rodents. Many become dormant when the environment becomes too unfavourable and the food supplies limited. They either hibernate or aestivate in their burrows; some do both. While inactive the ground squirrel lives off its 'savings'—a supply of fat accumulated during the times of plenty. Weight loss during this period can be phenomenal: woodchucks lose 35 to 50 per cent of their body weight during the four or five months they remain dormant. That unsociable sciurid, the thirteen-striped ground squirrel, can also reduce to about 60 per cent of its original body weight.

The red squirrel, one of the loveliest wild animals in Britain (*Bjorn Huseby*)

Tree squirrels do not hibernate, although some species live in areas where conditions can become severe. Most tree squirrels are tropical, and it is in the tropics that the largest and smallest of this extraordinary sub-family are found. Giant squirrels of the genus *Ratufa* approach 775mm (30in) in length, although over half of this is tail. These Ratu-fini are found in the Far East (southern India, Sri Lanka, the Malay Peninsula and the East Indies), and despite their size are fully arboreal. They are reddish-orange in colour and are said to be capable of leaps of up to 6m (20ft). At the other end of the scale the dwarf tree squirrel of the genus *Nannosciurus* is the smallest of all; it is less than 100mm (4in) in length, about the same size as a house mouse. Other squirrel species have a rather more dubious claim to fame. The Kaibab squirrel, *S. kaibabensis*, is isolated from its nearest relative by one of the world's greatest natural boundaries—the Grand Canyon of northern Arizona— and numbers no more than 1,000 animals. About the same size as the grey squirrel, this lovely creature possesses a grizzled grey coat except for its tail, which is startling white with an indistinct greyish stripe running along the centre of its upper side. The Kaibab squirrel is found only on the Kaibab Plateau, an area of some 70 by 30 miles. It feeds almost exclusively on the cambium layer of the yellow pine, and as this tree is said to habe deteriorated on the plateau, the population of the Kaibab squirrel may decrease even further.

Both ground and tree squirrels are active during daylight but the final sciurid group, the flying squirrels of Asia, North and Central America and eastern Europe, are nocturnal. They are seldom seen but emerge during late evening to feed upon fruits, seeds and insects. The flying squirrels have special folds of skin between wrist and ankle which, when extended, allow the animal to parachute for great distances. One species even possesses special muscles for moving the skin-wing folds during flight.

Bushy tail, plumed ears, big eyes and comic mannerisms (*Bjorn Huseby*)

Britain's Two Species

Britain and western Europe can boast none of these exotic beasts. There are no ground or flying squirrels within at least 1,000 miles of the British Isles. Only one species of tree squirrel is indigenous to our shores, the red squirrel, *Sciurus vulgaris*, (Linnaeus, 1758). Another, the American grey squirrel, *Sciuris carolinensis*, (Gmelin), also inhabits these islands and, although an alien, is probably better known than the British red. The grey has usurped the red over much of southern and central England, for reasons which are far from simple (see Chapter 4). It has also stolen the red squirrel's position in the nation's psyche; for instance, in a children's story book written and printed in the United Kingdom, every time a squirrel is figured in the drawings (eight times) it is undoubtedly the American variety. The grey squirrel is an interesting beast, but on the principle of first come, first served, in the next chapter our native species takes priority.

2
The Red Squirrel - The Native

DL 4/63 .

The family Sciuridae has been present in Europe since before the Miocene era (26 million years ago), making the squirrel as true an inhabitant of the British Isles as any of our mammals (Kurten, 1968). Because of their tree-living habits, few squirrel remains have become fossilised, but these are sufficient to reconstruct the events leading up to the establishment of the present British red-squirrel population.

The ancestor of the red squirrel is thought to have been an extinct type, *Sciurus whitei* (White's squirrel). Remains of *S.whitei* and *S. vulgaris*, our red squirrel, are known from the English Cromer Bed Series, which have been dated to as early as pre-glacial Pleistocene (about one million years ago). White's squirrel appears to have died out before the coming of the Ice Ages, leaving our own red squirrel as the only member of the tree-squirrel family in western Europe, a situation which remained unchanged until the artificial introduction of the American grey, *S.carolinensis* in the nineteenth century.

With the arrival of the Ice Ages, the glacial sheets spread southwards across almost all of the United Kingdom. Most probably no suitable habitat remained for squirrels anywhere on these islands, and we must assume that they either migrated southwards across the land bridge that then existed between Britain and continental Europe, or stayed on within the fast-diminishing forests and eventually became extinct. So, our present native red squirrel must have repopulated these islands from southern Europe following the retreat of the last ice sheet, 10-15,000 years ago. It was lucky for us that they did; the land bridge by which they crossed sank some 7,000 years ago, 'cutting off further invasion of land animals and leaving us without the number of species which our favourable climate and varied surface entitle us to' (Wallace, 1860).

Red squirrel (*Åke Lindau, Ardea Photographics*) ♀

It is incredible that a creature as small and seemingly delicate as the red squirrel could have survived these hardships. Yet it is very successful, with a range covering most of Eurasia, from Britain to Japan and from northern Russia to the Indian sub-continent. Within this huge range the red squirrel has developed into a number of subspecies, each differing slightly in size or morphology. Zoologists distinguish between these closely related groups by tacking a third Latinised name onto the specific name, *Sciurus vulgaris*. Sometimes they get a little carried away; Ellerman and Morrison-Scott (1951) recognise as many as forty-two subspecies of red squirrel! As most of these are based on variations in the squirrel's fur colour (a feature known to differ even within the same region), such a huge number of varieties seems unwarranted. In the British Isles there is but one endemic subspecies—the so-called light-tailed squirrel, *Sciurus vulgaris leucorus* (Kerr, 1972). 'True' subspecies inhabiting regions adjacent to the British Isles are: *Sciurus vulgaris vulgaris* of southern Scandinavia, *S.v.varius* of arctic Scandinavia, and *S.v.fuscoater* of the north-west European coast. Introductions of these European subspecies over the past 100 years have probably diluted the blood of our native stock.

Bright-eyed and Bushy-tailed

In its summer coat the British red squirrel is one of the most beautiful of our native mammals, with big black eyes, long tail and comic mannerisms. It is smaller than the introduced grey squirrel, with a head and body length of approximately 219mm (8.6in). The tail, at 182mm (7.2in), is almost as long as head and body put together. Its weight is notoriously variable, changing markedly with locality and food abundance, but is on average about 300g (10.6oz) for both sexes, though the male is said to be slightly heavier than the female. Both sexes have noticeable plumes on their long pointed ears: these function in social communication (see Chapter 6). The tail is bushy, has hair on both sides and is used, like the ears, in social displays. When they first leave the drey, young squirrels possess neither ear plumes nor bushy tail. Hairs on the adult tail may be anything up to 100mm (3.9in) in length and are parted in the middle, as they are in dormice.

When the animal sits, it usually lays its tail up over its back, though when in the drey during cold weather it may wrap the tail around its body like a fur stole. And, as Topsell wrote; 'as peacocks cover themselves with their tails in hot weather from the rage of the sun as under a shadow, with the same disposition doth the squirrel cover her body against heat . . .' In fact the name squirrel derives from the diminutive form of the Latin *sciurus*, which is itself borrowed from *skiouros*, an ancient Greek word meaning 'shadow tail'.

Acting as a defence against the weather is not the only function of a bushy tail. In climbing, leaping and swimming it is held straight out as a balancing rod; it is swung from side to side whenever a squirrel tries to balance on the thin topmost branches of a tree; and, equally important, it is used as the signalling flag in a complicated semaphore system informing other squirrels of its owners' emotions and intentions.

The hindlegs of the red squirrel are longer and much more powerful than the forelegs (fig 2). The 'hands' have four long digits with high,

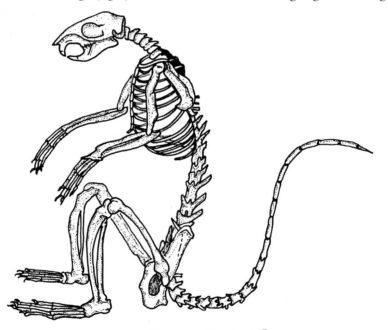

2. Skeleton of squirrel

round, sharp claws set close together. The thumb is involuted, almost vetigial, with a small flattened nail. When the squirrel eats a nut the digits are spread and held curved, pressing the nut against the tiny tubercle of the thumb. In the hind limbs, all five 'toes' are developed and all bear curved claws. Digit one is the shortest, three and four the longest, and two and five of intermediate length.

The squirrel is particularly well-endowed with vibrissae (whiskers) and other tactile hairs. There are four sets on the head: the usual 'nose' whiskers, one group above and one below the eyes, and a small number just in front of the throat on the underside of the head. Similar hairs are also found at the roots of all four feet, on the outer sides of the forelegs and on the underside of the body, as well as at the root of the tail. These hairs act like the antennae of insects or the 'feelers' of slugs and snails; they give advance warning of objects before the rest of the squirrel's body makes contact. With such an early-warning system, the squirrel is able to move easily along the swaying highways of branches.

Tail, limbs and whiskers are all ideally adapted for a tree-living way of life. Wolfgang Gewalt described its climbing ability:

The animal goes up tree trunks quickly and surely, moving with a jerky motion as it characteristically puts the claws of both fore feet or both hind feet into the bark and then pushes. The squirrel balances easily on rough, swinging branches. When it wants to jump to the top of a neighbouring tree, it gets as close to that tree as it can; this puts the squirrel out on the peripheral branches of the tree from which it will jump; there the animal crouches, a hesitant and unhappy figure. Because the squirrel cannot make a powerful spring from such a support, it loses much of the height of its jump, thus landing in a much lower location in the neighbouring tree. The squirrel climbs down the trunk headfirst, sticking the claws of its hind feet (which are stretched as far to the rear as possible) into the bark of the tree, as supports; then the animal loosens this anchor and moves its fore legs forward to a new grip position, consequently moving down the tree in a jerky 'hop-slide' motion.

It advances over open ground between trees in graceful jumps but with many stops, usually on high ground or a tree stump, half raising its body and peering around carefully for signs of danger.

Colour Forms

The red-squirrel coat in winter is brownish-grey above with the underparts white, as with most day-living arboreal animals. The light underparts, being a similar colour to the sky, help to camouflage the squirrel from the eyes of ground predators. The hairs of the tail are thick and blackish, becoming dark brown with time. As the weeks pass by, the whole winter coat bleaches, becoming steadily paler, a phenomenon seen only in the British subspecies. The body fur moults twice each year, in spring and autumn, and the spring moult puts an end to the bleaching process on limbs, head and trunk. But the hairs of the tail and ear tufts are lost only once a year, during the autumn moult; these parts of the body continue to bleach throughout spring and summer so that some squirrels have pale-yellow tails and ear tufts from June. A few have tails of almost pure white and well deserve their soubriquet, light-tailed squirrel. When first observed, this feature was not thought to occur generally in Britain. Not until the late 1800s when Thomas published a paper on the moult of the British red squirrel did zoologists accept the bleaching process as a countrywide phenomenon, unique to the British Isles.

Tail-bleaching distinguishes the British red squirrel from its closest continental relative, *S.v.vulgaris* (Linnaeus). But there are other differences, chief amongst them being the absence of polymorphism in the British variety. Over much of its geographical range the fur of the red squirrel shows two main colour phases (light and dark) with a range of intermediate forms. The two colour types are not species, or even subspecies, they interbreed freely and, despite the fact that they often inhabit the same forest, the colour forms show a relatively stable distribution within a given area. Such 'balanced polymorphism' is not unique to the red squirrel; it is seen in many mammals and also some birds. For example, the St Vincent parrot, *Amazona guildingii*, an endangered species which occurs only on the small Caribbean island of St Vincent, has orange and green forms which nest and breed together. It seems that the balance between colour forms is held stable because

Red squirrel (*Åke Lindau, Ardea Photographics*)

each possesses certain advantages (which the other lacks), during certain stages of development or in a particular part of the habitat.

Work on the red squirrel in Denmark, Poland, Germany and Russia (Mortensen, 1965; Zawoizka, 1958; Lühring, 1928; Ognev, 1940) showed a definite correlation of the dark phase with high altitude, heavy rainfall and spruce, fir and beech woodlands. In contrast, the light phase was associated with low altitude, low rainfall and pine woodlands.

At first it was believed that altitude, rainfall and perhaps other meteorological factors were important in the 'production' of the different colour phases. This hypothesis suffered a severe blow when it was shown that in Denmark, on the island of Fyn, there were exclusively dark-phase squirrels despite the fact that the island is of low altitude and light rainfall (Spärck, 1936). The consensus today is that vegetation broadly determines the colour phase, with the light variety being associated with pine forest. This theory appears to explain the absence of the dark phase in the United Kingdom, where the primary habitat of the red squirrel is *Pinus sylvestris* (Scots pine) forest.

Nevertheless, although the distribution and numbers of the red squirrel in Britain suggest it prefers mature conifer woodland, it will also inhabit mixed and deciduous mature woodlands; in Scotland, for example, it can be found in the broad-leaved forests of Argyll and Aberdeenshire. This seems to upset the new 'pine-forest-equals-light-phase-squirrel' theory, and we will have to wait for the results of future research before the question of polymorphism in the red squirrel can be satisfactorily resolved.

As well as balanced polymorphism, melanic (black) and albino (white) squirrels are known, both in the British Isles and abroad. The melanic form is by far the rarest in Britain, although in certain districts of Switzerland, France and Germany it is said to be fairly common. Shorten (1954) mentions three separate observations of black squirrels: in Norfolk during 1944, Cheshire in 1951, and County Down, Ireland, in 1950. Epping Forest was also said to harbour 'black' red squirrels until at least 1947, when the American grey squirrel arrived. Shorten believes that the majority of British melanic squirrels derive from continental introductions, although there is no real reason to suppose that melanism is somehow restricted to 'non-British' varieties of *S.vulgaris*. One of the earliest records of a British melanic was that of M. R. Pryor, who related that in 1865 '. . . while shooting near Watford I distinctly saw a black squirrel . . . but not knowing they were not often seen in England I did not shoot it.' So much for the English sportsman. Woe betide those unfortunate rarities which Mr Pryor knew to be scarce!

Albinism is far better documented and much more common. Over a period of 23 years Barrett-Hamilton records 10 pure white, pink-eyed squirrels, and 1 piebald animal. Shorten mentions 5 albino squirrels from Wales; when a female from these was mated with a normal-coloured male, she produced a litter of three red young. Albinos are also reported from other parts of the country, for example Bidston Woods in Cheshire, while W. A. Cadman claimed to have seen stuffed albino squirrels at a pub in Bedale, North Yorkshire. Of the two freak types, the albino probably has the worst of it. The dark-phase squirrels of Europe are not too far removed from the melanic forms, and as the former so obviously thrive we might expect their darker cousins to do almost as well. Such a rosy future cannot be prophesied for the white specimens of the red squirrel; except perhaps in winter, when their white colouration may help to mask their presence, the albino squirrel is in deep trouble. When alarmed, a squirrel often lies completely immobile, hugging the bough of the tree on which it is sitting and relying on its coat colour to render it invisible among the leafy branches. But in such conditions the albino will stand out like a Caucasian at a Hottentot convention, making the poor beast easy picking for a predator. It is not known how long albino squirrels survive in the wild, but it is a fair guess that their life-span rarely equals that of their brown relatives.

Squirrels in Legend and History

White, black or more usually red, *Sciurus vulgaris* has been known to man from earliest times. Its mannerisms and attractive behaviour have resulted in a wealth of folk-tales and aphorisms. The squirrel has been associated with (amongst other attributes) curiosity, grace, nimbleness, thrift, speed and timidity. In heraldry, the image of a squirrel typifies a sylvan retirement, away from the world of men, to a quiet meditative life amongst the natural world. Derived, perhaps, from similar origins, the motif of a squirrel cracking a nut symbolises the maxim that in the search for truth one should pierce the husk of the external.

The squirrel was particularly important in Indo-Germanic mythology. In an Indian version of Amor and Psyche, a squirrel plays the part of the gnome, and in one Indian epic it soaks up the ocean with its tail. The squirrel's colour caused it to become sacred to the god Donar, the simple-minded though brutal thunder-god of the Teutons, whose colour was red. Such pagan associations may have been responsible for the ritual hunting of red squirrels practised during the early Christian era. By killing squirrels, the faithful affirmed their belief in Christianity and hoped somehow to harm the false god Donar. In Norse mythology, the squirrel appears as a deity messenger on the great ash tree, Yggdrasil. At the top of the tree sat a wise eagle, symbolising life, while in its roots was the corpse-eating serpent, Niddhogg. The squirrel ran between these two impressive creatures, carrying insulting messages and generally trying to stir up trouble!

As well as figuring in myth and legend, the red squirrel was kept both as pet and food animal in historical times. As pets, they were especially treasured by the ladies of Imperial Rome. It seems they were also beloved of children, for in a graveyard near the Hungarian Lake Balaton, Lipp found the remains of five children each of which had on one shoulder the skeleton of a squirrel, presumably sacrificed to keep its owner company in the afterlife. Although such instances are rare, the pet squirrel, whether Roman or Hungarian, had a very cushy number indeed. Not so those squirrels in the forests of western Europe. Prehistoric man found him not so much cute plaything as tasty morsel: squirrel bones have been found in the remains of several lake-built villages in Switzerland and there is little doubt *S. vulgaris* figured on the menu of these lake dwellers.

Happily, we no longer glory in the culinary delights of freshly roasted red squirrel. We prefer our native species 'on the hoof'. But for many people, roasting is too good a fate to bestow on our next subject, the introduced American grey squirrel.

3
The Grey Squirrel - The Invader

The original home of the American grey squirrel *Sciuris carolinensis* (Gmelin) is the dense hardwood forests of eastern Canada and the United States, from Ontario and New Brunswick down to Florida. There are five races recognised in North America, and our grey squirrel shows characteristics that indicate it derives primarily from a mixture of the most southerly and most northerly of the five races, *S. c. carolinensis* and *S. c. leucotis*.

S. carolinensis carolinensis, Gmelin. The southern gray squirrel. A large arboreal squirrel with long, flat, bushy tail; ears usually without tufts; prevailing color of upper parts grayish. Sexes colored alike; seasonal variation not conspicuous. Upper parts mixed gray and yellowish-brown, head and back darker and with more of a brownish tinge than sides of limbs, neck and rump, which are grayish; ears yellowish-white; hairs of tail yellowish at base, banded with black, tipped with white, the general impression being blackish overlaid with white. Under parts whitish. Immature much like adults, but with less yellowish-brown. Sexes of equal size. Total length 18 in., tail vertebrae 8.5 in., hind foot 2.5 in. Soles of feet usually naked. Distribution (after Miller 1900): north from Florida to about the lower Hudson Valley, west through the Alleghenies south of Pennsylvania to Indiana, Missouri, Oklahoma, and the edge of the plains.

S. carolinensis leucotis, Gapper. Larger and grayer than typical *carolinensis*, apt to occur in black or melanistic phase; soles of feet may be hairy in winter. Upper parts in winter, silvery-gray with faint grizzling of yellowish-brown on head, back, and upper surfaces of hands and feet; under parts white. Summer pelage with more rusty brown, especially along sides. Melanistic phase, everywhere black; various degrees of

31

intergradation between gray and black phases may occur. Total length 20 in.; tail vertebrae 9.2 in.; hind foot 2.8 in. Distribution (after Miller, 1900): Transition Zone and locally lower edge of Canadian Zone from the Alleghenies of Pennsylvania and southern Ontario; west to Minnesota.

(Anthony, 1928)

The American grey squirrel of Britain is easily distinguished from our native variety by its speckled grey coat and white underparts. As with the red squirrel, both melanic (black) and albino (white) forms occasionally arise in its population. Apart from very slight tufting in summer, the grey lacks pronounced ear tufts and has a markedly less bushy tail than its British cousin's. In England, as in America, it is happiest in open woodland or parks, even suburban back gardens, but unfortunately for the red squirrel, the grey does not seem limited to these areas. It will also nest and breed in the red's favourite habitat—coniferous plantations —provided there are seed-bearing hardwoods nearby. The grey also prefers to live at lower altitudes, a choice which reflects its original home on the eastern seaboard of America.

In North America, the grey squirrel is an integral part of the Ne-arctic fauna. Americans, both Indian and white, have known of its existence for a very long time, long enough for strange superstitions and remedies to take root. In some States, the squirrel is found in the role of the English black cat: if it happens to cross your path then bad luck will surely follow. Alive, it may be the harbinger of doom, but when dead various parts of its body are said to be indispensable for a variety of ailments, even for magic. For example: 'To keep a baby from having serious trouble cutting its teeth, rub its gums with the brains of a squirrel.' After a treatment like that, I doubt if the baby would have any more trouble with anything! Less obnoxious but equally intriguing is the ritual to be carried out by lonesome squirrel-hunters (or presumably anyone else who can beg, borrow or filch a dead squirrel). When you kill a squirrel, pull out its teeth, and put them under your pillow saying:

> Ninny, ninny, little squirrel
> That chatters in the tree,
> Tell me who my true love is to be.

32

Grey squirrel (*Dennis Avon & Tony Tilford, Ardea Photographics*) ?

How this incantation works, or why the poor squirrel should want to help, and not punish, its murderers is not explained. Or perhaps the future spouse *is* the punishment!

The Introduction of the Grey

In Britain, the grey squirrel has not been around long enough to be the subject of superstitions, so the animal is useless even for folk-magic. It is hard to condone the actions of those who struggled long and hard to establish the species on these islands. Did they give no thought to the damage it might do, to the fate of the native red squirrel, or to the potential loss to trees and other vegetation? It has been suggested, in mitigation, that those concerned believed the grey squirrel would be (as it was in America) an aesthetic addition to the fauna of the British countryside. But it was already common knowledge that the smaller red squirrel could cause extensive damage to tree plantations—from 1835 (over forty years before the first recorded introduction of the grey squirrel) attempts were made to control it. It seems strange that these misguided meddlers in our native fauna could not predict a similar, or worse scenario arising out of the introduction of an alien form.

Sightings of grey squirrels at Llandisilio Hall, Denbighshire, were made as early as 1828, and in a letter to the *Cambrian Quarterly Magazine*'s editor, dated 1830, it was stated that for some time before 1830 there were grey squirrels at three sites in Montgomeryshire. Presuming the identification to be correct, these animals must have derived from an early introduction by a person or persons unknown. The fate of these animals is likewise obscure.

The first known release of *Sciurus carolinensis* into the English countryside was by T. V. Brocklehurst in 1876. This worthy set at liberty one pair of grey squirrels in Henbury Park, near Macclesfield, Cheshire. It is not known what became of this couple, though possibly they became established. A pair of grey squirrels shot at Highfields in Nottinghamshire in 1884—more than thirty-five miles away—may have derived from the original pair. More likely, they came from some undocumented release. The second known attempt at introduction—of five grey squirrels at Bushy Park, Middlesex by G. S. Page in 1889—

Red squirrels—the one below visits an already-barked trunk (*B. S. Turner*)

was also abortive. But Mr Page was nothing if not persistent. A scant twelve months later he imported a further ten grey squirrels from the USA, which were released at Woburn Abbey by the 9th Duke of Bedford. Perhaps because of their larger number, these settled down in the abbey grounds and increased. Soon they were seen in the surrounding countryside, the first truly successful introduction in the British Isles. By 1920 the squirrels of Woburn had populated an area of 1,350 square miles around the original release point.

In 1902 an unnamed American was responsible for the next release, this time of 100 animals at Kingston Hill, Richmond Park, Surrey. Two successful releases were bad enough, but soon the practice of helping the grey invader as much as possible seemed to take on all the characteristics of a fad. From 1902 until 1929 there was an explosion in both the number and location of squirrel introductions. The main 'villain of the piece' was once again Woburn Abbey. In 1903, 1906 and twice in 1908, animals trapped at Woburn were sent to other areas for release. Grey squirrels were also sent from Woburn to London Zoo between 1905 and 1907 whence they were distributed to at least three other centres (Appendix 1). In all, Woburn was responsible for nine grey squirrel introductions (possibly more) in other parts of Britain. The complete list of introductions after 1902 is given in Appendix 1.

In Scotland the grey squirrel found almost instant success. A single pair, liberated in 1892 at Finnart on the shore of Loch Long on the borders of Dunbartonshire and Argyllshire, survived and began to increase. Eleven years later the descendents of this rodent Adam and Eve had already spread northwards from their point of release to Arrochar and Tarbert. By 1906 they had reached Inverberg, by 1907 Garelochead and in 1912, twenty years after the first release, they had spread as far south as Culdross, a full twenty miles from the initial point of liberation. Soon (1915) they had established themselves in Stirlingshire, their range at this time measuring over 300 square miles, an average increase of 12 square miles each year! In Ireland progress was slow but just as sure. Once again, the squirrels of Woburn were shunted across the country to seed a hitherto untouched part of the

Grey squirrel eating young horse-chestnut leaves (*F. V. Blackburn*)

37

British Isles. A release of eight *S.carolinensis* at Castle Forbes, County Longford, in 1913 by the Earl of Granard resulted in a continuing spread until by 1956 they had reached Fermanagh, Armagh, Tyrone and County Down.

The Grey's Relentless March

It is depressing to read the detailed accounts of the grey squirrel's march through the United Kingdom. Despite the fact that by 1931 a further 8,500 square miles had been added to its range (making, *in toto*, a bridgehead of at least 10,000 square miles), very little had been done to eradicate, or even hold in check, the grey squirrel's steadily swelling numbers. However in that same year it seemed that nature herself was taking a hand: the grey population steadied and then began to drop. Some form of epidemic disease swept through the species' strongholds and diseased squirrels were found in at least five counties, ranging from Berkshire northwards to Yorkshire. With the population so low, this surely was the time to attempt to wipe out the invading species. But the authorities did nothing, and within a few years grey-squirrel numbers had returned to their pre-disease levels, and their range had even increased. By 1937, the numerous small squirrel 'islands' of earlier years had coalesced into nine main areas in which the grey squirrel reigned supreme. These were south-east England and the Midlands; Yorkshire (including a small southern part of Durham); Cheshire, with overflows into small areas of Denbighshire, Shropshire and Flintshire; a southern coastal strip extending from Poole to Southampton; Devon; Dumbarton; Fife; and a single Irish centre at Castle Forbes in County Longford.

Grey Squirrels Prohibition Order

At last the authorities made a move. The Grey Squirrels Prohibition of Importation and Keeping Order, 1937, made it illegal for anyone to bring a grey squirrel into this country from abroad, or to catch and keep the species as a pet. This piece of legislation rates as a classic example of bureaucratic inertia. Had the Order been made law twenty

Grey squirrel (*Dennis Avon & Tony Tilford, Ardea Photographics*)

years earlier, there might have been some chance of checking the grey squirrel, but by 1937 it was a case of shutting the cage door after the squirrel had bolted and bred! This Act is still in force, although widely flouted. While preparing this book, I have met several individuals, and in one case a prestigious film group, who were keeping grey squirrels. Some were even attempting to breed them.

Nevertheless, the 1937 Order was a step in the right direction. Unfortunately, within two years England was embroiled in World War II and such trivial matters as the grey squirrel had to take a back seat. By 1954 it had reached Cornwall and Cardiganshire, and the main Scottish centres above had coalesced. Despite a second population crash in 1955—due to failure of the food supply—which left the population at only one-third the level of the previous year, the greys slowly increased their hold on more counties. By the early 1960s, it was easier to say where greys were absent. There are still areas of Wales which have never seen it. In England, the counties of Cumbria and northern Lancashire have yet to see the speckled grey pelt, and in the east of the country, northern Essex, Suffolk and parts of Norfolk are still free. This is probably because the grey menace has difficulty in making its way into these areas. Despite the proximity of Yorkshire and Cheshire, both with thriving squirrel populations, Lancashire remained squirrel-less for many years. Shorten (1962) has attributed this to geographical barriers such as the River Mersey, the high ground of the Pennine Hills and the industrial conurbations of southern Lancashire.

Certain topographical features do slow down the spread of *S. carolinensis*. The low-lying fens of eastern England helped prevent the passage of grey-squirrel migrants into East Anglia. Similarly, the treeless Highlands of Scotland have confined the species to the lowland areas and therefore greatly decreased the colonisation rate there.

It is hard not to be impressed by the resilience of the alien invader, not to have a sneaking regard for its ability to move through totally foreign habitat, to negotiate rivers, marshlands and roadways, and still to thrive. It is known that squirrels forced to migrate from their normal area of habitation rarely survive, yet the grey is still with us, and is increasing. It is obviously a heroic little beast. But we come back to

40

the fact that, as the grey population increased, that of the native red squirrel waned. Why?

At just over 457mm (1ft 6in) long, the grey squirrel tops the red by at least 76mm (3in), and with a weight of 510-567g (18-20oz) it is far heavier than the red. It is also a far more aggressive and powerful animal, which has been observed to fight and kill rats, rabbits, leverets and even as powerful a predator as the stoat. Apart from its teeth, the grey defends itself with its long, powerful legs; used together, the hind limbs can disembowel a would-be attacker. It has been known to dispatch cockerels and sitting birds, or to take and eat their eggs. On occasion, fledglings are attacked, although Shorten (1954) thinks such assaults are the result of the chicks' heads reminding the squirrel of a nut. This may be true, as most deaths are caused by the squirrel cracking open the cranium of the unfortunate nestlings.

There are also records of grey killing grey, or grey killing red. This latter activity has been cited to explain the rise of the grey squirrel in England and what seems to be a corollary, the decline of the red. But whether such 'genocide' is common within the grey-squirrel population itself, or is perpetrated as a strategy for ridding the greys of their smaller relatives are other questions, ones which we must consider very carefully in the next chapter.

4
Grey versus Red

The grey squirrel is increasing in the British Isles, spreading its range, while the red squirrel shrinks into an ever-smaller area. One has only to compare the maps (fig 3) to see the enormous change in relative abundance between the two species. What is questionable is *why* the change has occurred. There are a number of theories, ranging from simple direct murder of the red by the grey to a complex and extremely subtle combination of factors which, in sum, have tipped the balance against the red.

The idea of active 'premeditated' genocide is based partly on observation and partly on anthropomorphic assumptions. When men push back other men from territory they have previously occupied, aggression usually plays a big part—we call it war. So if one squirrel species takes over from another, it may seem 'commonsense' to assume that they do so by force. But in biology, as in other sciences, commonsense should be used only as a jumping-off point, a preliminary hypothesis to be checked by the evidence of meticulous observation. So what does the evidence show?

In other parts of the globe, introduced animals have attacked and killed members of the indigenous fauna. The best-known example of this is man's introduction of placental mammals such as the fox and rabbit to the Australian mainland, where until then marsupial (pouched) mammals had held sway. The placental mammals (to which we ourselves belong) evolved after the marsupials, and were so much more efficient that, with the exception of the American oppossum, they wiped out their older cousins on every continent other than Australia, which is now the marsupials' last redoubt. As Australia was cut off from the rest of the world before the placentals evolved, this huge island became a sort of natural laboratory where the marsupial mammals could continue to evolve as if they were still top of the biological tree. But as soon as man's rabbits, foxes and goats arrived on the scene, many of the less efficient marsupial species found the competition too severe and gradually became extinct. On a large land mass like Australia the process of extinction takes many years but elsewhere, especially on

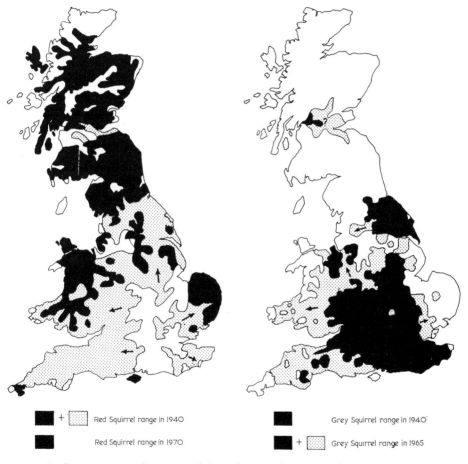

■ + ▦ Red Squirrel range in 1940

■ Red Squirrel range in 1970

■ Grey Squirrel range in 1940

■ + ▦ Grey Squirrel range in 1965

3. (*Left*) Decrease in the range of the red squirrel *Sciurus vulgaris* since 1940 (*Right*) Increase in the British range of the American grey squirrel *Sciurus carolinensis* since 1940 (From Shorten 1962, Tittensor 1970, 1975)

43

small islands, extermination may be rapid. Numerous species of Pacific rail, for example those of Chatham and Wake Islands, were destroyed within a few years by the introduction of alien species. Even today the process is continuing; several species of Caribbean lizard have been blotted out by the release of pet cats, which take up a feral existence and find that the lizards are easy pickings.

Britain may be larger than most Pacific islands, but it is still a relatively small piece of the globe, especially when compared with Australia. Therefore the idea that an American, alien, species could be killing off the native red squirrel was very plausible, the more so when, at first, observation confirmed it. Douglas Middleton (1931), one of the first to amass information on this topic, recorded several eye-witness accounts of grey/red interactions, mainly from southern England. Several combats were witnessed in Hertfordshire and on one occasion, after driving off the grey, a red squirrel was found dying from wounds to the throat. Similar activity occurred at Brasted in Kent, and Burnham in Somerset. In the north of the country, Middleton recorded that a grey was seen eating several young red squirrels, and that dead red squirrels were found under trees containing dreys of the American species. Shorten (1962) states that a 'fairly typical comment might run':

> I remember when I was a boy there used to be red squirrels all over the place, hundreds of them. Not just in the plantations, either: we used to see them down here in the village too. But as soon as the grey squirrel came—though that's more like a rat, not a squirrel—all the reds just vanished. They were just slaughtered. I've heard that the grey ones used to castrate the others when they fought. The only red squirrel that I've seen lately was one that we shot a few years ago by mistake, and that looked more like a cross-breed. I don't believe that there are any real red squirrels left in the whole country.

The attacks have continued. A grey squirrel was seen to enter a red's drey at Whipsnade in 1946. It dropped two objects to the ground; they were retrieved and found to be dead young red squirrels, bitten in the neck. A similar report from Cheshire involved three young reds. Many accounts tell of red squirrels being chased by greys, the pursued animal sometimes screaming as it raced along the branches.

The 'Grey-kills-Red' Theory Does Not Hold

Yet against these tales of horror are observations in which grey and red squirrels are seen to practise a sort of peaceful co-existence. Keepers in Epping Forest in the early 1950s stated that grey and red fed in close proximity (sometimes as close as two yards) with no sign of aggression. They were said to forage together and even to take cover on the same branch. Fighting or chasing had never been observed in the forest. These observations have been verified in a PhD study conducted fifty-five miles to the north of Epping Forest, in the ancient forest of Thetford Chase in Norfolk, an area of red/grey interface—the first study directed primarily towards unravelling the mechanics of red-grey interaction. Its organiser, Jonathan Reynolds of the University of East Anglia, spent three years in the forest, sometimes working an eighteen-hour day. I accompanied this tall, slim and rather laconic biologist on his daily rounds, seeing both red and grey squirrels, visiting trap lines and marking the captive animals. As we walked, Jonathan said he had observed virtually no aggressive encounters in those parts of the wood frequented by both species. As in Epping Forest, greys and reds could be seen in close proximity, feeding, for example, in a completely mixed group in a forest clearing without any sign of interspecific aggression. Like most experts, he felt the grey-kills-red theory to be simplistic, and that we would have to explain both the grey squirrel's ascendancy and the red's decline in rather more subtle terms than simple aggression. Certainly, there are not enough recorded 'murders' to account for the rapid fall in numbers of the red squirrel.

Another Theory: The Grey as Disease-carrier

What then is the explanation? Some have suggested that the grey squirrel is the carrier of disease to the native species. This is a valid suggestion. Those irresponsible enough to liberate *Sciurus carolinensis* in the British Isles certainly took no pains to discover if it might harbour some disease fatal to our native British red squirrels. Very selective diseases which, while causing almost no effect in the carrier species, may decimate a closely related form which has had no time to build up immunity, are certainly not unknown. An example is the rabbit disease myxomatosis, a viral infection that can produce tumours of mucous or gelatinous tissue (mysomas) in the infected animal and which may lead ultimately to death. The virus is endemic amongst certain rabbit species of the Americas, for example the cottontail rabbits of the south-western states of the USA, but it rarely causes problems in this species. Had the cottontail been introduced into the British Isles in 1876 instead of the grey squirrel, then myxomatosis would undoubtedly have been rampant in these islands more than seventy-five years before it was (artificially) introduced.

The effect on British rabbits when the disease first hit their warrens was catastrophic: dying rabbits littered fields and roads all over the United Kingdom. Within a single year 99 per cent of British rabbits were dead. Such a case of interspecies infection is not unique; an even more disastrous example of genocide-by-disease occurred early in the twentieth century during the exploration of Christmas Island, near Indonesia. When Dr C. W. Andrews visited this Indian Ocean island in 1898 he found two indigenous species of rodent: Maclear's rat *Rattus macleari* and *R.nativitatus*, the bulldog rat. At this time both species were so plentiful that they were regarded as pests. Maclear's rat in particular visited human habitations regularly, 'entering the tents or shelters, running over the sleepers, and upsetting everything in their search for food' (Andrews, 1900). When Andrews returned to the island only eleven years later, both species were extinct. The settlement's medical officer, Dr McDougal, reported that around 1902 hundreds of rats were found dead and dying during daylight hours. Andrews investgated the reports and came to the conclusion that the introduced ship rat, *Rattus rattus* var (which had multiplied to considerable proportions on the island), had brought with it a blood disease to which the native species were vulnerable.

So the theory that greys infect red squirrels with some debilitating or fatal disease seems attractive. But there is no hard evidence of it. It is true that the grey squirrel is susceptible to most of the diseases that afflict the red—coccidiosis, for example, and probably mange. Grey squirrels could therefore infect red squirrels in the same way as greys infect greys (equally, reds could infect greys). But there is no evidence of any myxomatosis-like contagion to which the grey squirrel remains immune while transferring it to the red squirrel. Indeed the facts we have (Middleton, 1931) show that at times of rapid decline in red-squirrel numbers, those in areas with no grey squirrels are equally badly hit. So scientists looked more closely at what happened to the red-squirrel population in those years before the coming of the introduced American species. What they discovered threw a new light on the whole problem.

Since the retreat of the last glaciers the red squirrel has always been a part of the British fauna, but its population has nevertheless varied considerably over the years. Small decreases and increases occurred (and continue to occur) owing to the abundance or otherwise of its food resources. Larger fluctuations have also taken place, usually because of temporary epidemic diseases (epizootics), or widespread habitat destruction. Deforestation of the Scottish mainland during the late seventeenth century led to the almost total extinction of the Scottish red squirrel, but replanting of trees (and several introductions of English squirrels) resulted in a good recovery by the mid-1800s. By 1890, red squirrels were so numerous and so destructive that special 'squirrel clubs' were organised in an attempt to keep them in check. Although they no doubt helped to swell the coffers of cartridge-makers throughout the country, these clubs did little to reduce the number of squirrels in Scottish woods.

From around 1900 to 1930, there was a dramatic decline in red-squirrel numbers. The grey squirrel was not a force to be reckoned with during the early part of this period and, as mentioned, squirrel clubs had been plugging away at the red squirrel for years and had had no effect. The cause of this crash was an unknown disease or com-bination of diseases which took a heavy toll of red squirrels throughout the country.

Many people were so impressed with this decline that they still remembered it even after a space of forty years. Mr D. R. Parker, writing in 1953, stated:

From 1908 onwards I was one of five keepers on a large estate in south Devon where there were hundreds of them [red squirrels]—no grey ones.

47

In early December, 1912, they seemed to be getting scarcer; by Christmas there wasn't one to be seen . . . [we] went up to the dreys and in each we found a pair curled up dead. The fur was all off the hind part of the back, and the tail looked like a rat's; also the ear tufts were gone. It looked like the mange which we considered it was . . . It was the same for miles around on neighbouring estates; whatever the disease, it wiped them all out in a matter of a few weeks, and up to about three years ago not one had been seen on the estate. I haven't heard of any being seen around here.

Grey squirrels have now colonised the whole of Devon, including Mr Parker's estate.

Competition for Habitat—Red Loses Out

If the grey squirrel is not the vector of some infection fatal to the red squirrel, why should the latter continue to decline? The answer may lie in a theory proposed more than fifty years ago by an Austrian scientist, A. A. Gauss. His proposition was that where two species are dependent on the same habitat and the same resources for survival, one will perish in favour of the species which is better able to utilise or hold the territory for itself. So perhaps this is the answer; red and grey compete for certain areas in the UK and for a variety of reasons it is the red which loses out. On present evidence it does seem that, especially in hardwood or mixed forests, the needs of the two species are similar. Armed with this knowledge, and with what we know of the red squirrel's periodic fluctuation in numbers, it is possible to present a fairly plausible picture of the way in which the grey squirrel has ousted the red over great areas of the British countryside.

Before the introduction of *Sciurus carolinensis*, the red squirrel was the only herbivorous, arboreal mammal in the British Isles. It could therefore increase and decrease as it 'wished'. The woods were always there to recolonise when its numbers began to rise, and there was no danger that some other species might be found 'squatting' on what had previously been red-squirrel territory. But the coming of the grey squirrel changed all that. The reds were faced with a competitor bigger and stronger than themselves, and probably also more able to adapt its behaviour to suit changing circumstances. Such changes were already occurring during the years of grey-squirrel introductions: the increased spread of conurbations, alteration of agricultural practices, etc.

If the grey and red were found together in the same location at the same time there was very little *overt* interspecific aggression (we have already seen this in, for example, the Jonathan Reynolds' study). But the greys may have exerted more subtle pressures on the red, so slowly reducing their numbers. They probably did not even have to resort to any offensive behaviour. All they had to do was wait for one of the periodic drops in the red squirrel's numbers, and then take over the whole of the area vacated by them. As the red squirrel's decline is often due to food shortage, we must assume that the grey squirrel is in some way better able to cope with this; we know that it forages more on the ground than does the red, so perhaps it is better able to survive failures of the nut and seed crops. As the reds begin once again to increase in numbers, they attempt to recolonise these areas they once shared but which are now full to capacity (or almost so) with big hungry greys. We shall see in Chapter 6 that squirrels are very territorial, especially against newcomers, so that most 'migrants' trying to establish a territory in a previously occupied area fail to survive (Thompson, 1977).

The red squirrel is therefore in trouble when it tries to re-enter its old stamping grounds; greys will not tolerate new greys, and they definitely will not let a red squirrel stay. Faced with its more powerful cousin, the red has no choice but to leave. But where can it go? There is no land available to support it. The red squirrel loses all ways—it makes no difference whether the decrease in its numbers is long or short term: whether piecemeal or on a larger scale, if the greys can move in first another area will be lost to the red squirrel.

By keeping the red squirrel out of land in which it could live and prosper, the grey is effectively 'killing off' red-squirrel overflow populations, the pioneering reds that have left the overcrowded conifer plantations in which they were born. The American invader may not kill its relative in battles to the death (the number destroyed in this way is very small) but, being deprived of *lebensraum*, the reds are killed just as surely as if they had been savaged. It is rather like a human tribe 'owning' a desert oasis and, with little overt force and even less homicide, preventing a second tribe from using the waterhole. Without water the second tribe is doomed, and without habitat the migrating reds likewise face extinction.

There is no doubt that most of the deciduous woodland now inhabited by grey squirrels is perfectly suitable for our native species. For approximately 6,000 years after the Ice Age, the only conifers England possessed were yew and juniper, yet the red squirrel thrived. In Europe, Spärck (1936) believes that the red squirrels of Fünen and West Zeeland, which survive perfectly well in deciduous woodland, have done so for at least 2,000 and perhaps as long as 3,000 years. In many ways it is fortunate that the nineteenth century saw such an upturn in the planting of conifers by man—without these sanctums the red squirrel might already have become extinct.

Man's Part in the Red's Defeat

So far we have assumed that the grey squirrel is totally to blame for the destruction of the red. This is definitely not the case. In most matters zoological the answers are not of the simple 'he-fell-'cos-I-pushed-him' kind. More often a multitude of factors have contributed to a 'fall'. In the fall of the red squirrel one of these factors has undoubtedly been man. Not all animal species are possessed of the same temperament; some may tolerate massive intrusions in their habitat whilst others the birds desert the whole area. This extreme intolerance to change from what they regard as normal can seriously affect their behaviour, perhaps upsetting the breeding cycle and so resulting in a disastrous drop in numbers. The most extreme example of such sensitivity.to change were probably the Moho birds of the Hawaiian Islands. These birds were so sensitive that a single jungle track cut in otherwise virgin forest filled with Moho food and nesting sites was sufficient to make the birds desert the whole area. This extreme intolerance to changes together with man's hunting for the bird's beautiful plumage, has resulted in the extinction of three of the four Moho species, with the fourth surviving only in extremely small numbers.

By all accounts the grey squirrel has nothing to fear from intrusion by man. It is made of sterner stuff than the red: bigger, stronger and probably more resistant to disease, it is also more robust emotionally. It can easily survive quite traumatic disturbances of its habitat, and seems able to make a living even in small sparse woodlands. The native red species is far less able to adjust to intrusion. It may be then, that the decreases in the red-squirrel population derive partly from the inroads our industrialised society has made into the quiet of rural Britain. Very few areas of the British Isles are extensively wooded, and even fewer are truly remote (this is especially true of England). Each weekend thousands of people leave the cities for the country, tramping through woodlands, talking, shouting, playing their portable radios and shattering the peace of the countryside. If red squirrels are as sensitive as I have suggested, they are likely to vacate such 'humanised' woodlands, or at least place them low on their list of desirable residences.

Many authors have stated that, by living in coniferous forest, the red squirrel has returned to its principal habitat, in which the grey does not seem able to survive. But, as we have seen, the red squirrel's primary home for more than 5,000 years was the natural deciduous woodland of most of Britain. It is, or can be, as much at home in hardwood as in pinewood forest. Until now we have assumed that the sole reason the red no longer holds these oak, beech and birch forests is because the grey in some way prevents its entry. But it is interesting that almost all the remaining strongholds of the red squirrel are not only coniferous, they are also prohibited to most humans, or so inaccessible that few people make the effort to visit them. Perhaps we make more impact on the red squirrel than we would care to admit. The grey squirrel makes a useful scapegoat, but it is probably not totally to blame.

Chemical Sprays

There is a final problem which, as far as I know, has yet to be recognised by conservationists. The coniferous forest in which the red squirrel lives is economically valuable and is subjected to many chemical sprays in an attempt to increase yield. At least one of these chemicals, 2,4,5,T (a relative of dioxin), has been shown to increase stillbirths and miscarriages in human mothers living close to sprayed areas. It is very likely that spraying conifers with 2,4,5,T has produced much the same effect on the red-squirrel females (who live *in* the sprayed area and are consequently exposed to heavier concentrations of chemical) and that the decline in red-squirrel numbers can be traced, at least in part, to this chemical contamination.

Last Refuge: Coniferous Forests

One trace of silver lining relieves the almost unremitting gloom of this chapter: it is doubtful that the grey squirrel will completely eliminate the red in Britain. The grey has not yet learned to survive exclusively in large unbroken stands of coniferous trees. The red squirrel can utilise this sort of habitat very well indeed, provided the trees are old enough to crop (over thirty-five years of age). There are now 4,215,000 acres of such forest planted, of which a little under 2,000,000 acres are old enough to support a red-squirrel population. Thanks to continued planting the figure in 1988 will be far higher. So, provided the resourceful *Sciurus carolinensis* does not find some way of exploiting coniferous forest, the native species seems reasonably safe.

Unfortunately there have been several disturbing reports of the grey squirrel turning to cone-bearing trees for an important segment of its food supply. If this is so, and the grey begins to move into completely coniferous forest, our native red squirrel is in the greatest danger of extinction, for it will certainly be slowly squeezed out of these last strongholds by the stronger alien.

When each of the two tree-squirrel species keeps to 'its own' habitat, the grey to broad-leaved and the red to coniferous forest, it is possible to view the introduction of the grey in terms of profit rather than loss. After all, we now have two species where there was but one. But it would be a zoological tragedy if we had to substitute our delicate—and unique—subspecies for the heavy-set and less attractive grey.

A grey descending a tree: it sticks its hind claws into the bark, loosens their grip and 'moves its forelegs forwards . . . consequently moving down the tree in a jerky hop-slide motion' (*E. T. Jones*) ?

Young grey squirrel eating (*A. J. Bond*)

5
Food and Home

Trees provide the squirrel with all it needs to survive. They give a safe refuge from most predators, an ideal place for a nest and, most important of all, an almost unlimited supply of food. Without trees the squirrel would be like a rat without a bolt-hole—very vulnerable to predators and not long for this world. Equally important, it would have to compete with such fellow rodents as rats for all the necessities of survival and in the face of these intelligent and aggressive relatives, it would almost certainly go to the wall.

All squirrels are primarily herbivorous; more correctly they are granivores, seed-eaters. Just what they do eat, and in what proportion, is usually determined by close observation. The squirrel grinds its food so thoroughly that an analysis of its stomach contents is all but impossible—all that is left are a few plant cells. One can make slides of the stomach contents and then try to identify the plants consumed by comparing the plant cells from the squirrel's stomach with a specially prepared slide series of all plants from the squirrel's habitat. However, having tried to unravel the mysteries of the menu of a woodmouse (*Apodemus sylvaticus*) using the same method, I believe that one can make as accurate an assessment blindfold with a list of all plant species and a bent pin. Direct observation of the squirrel's eating habits is much to be preferred (Appendix 2).

The Red Squirrel's Diet

Dr Andrew Tittensor's observations of both captive and wild red squirrels in Scotland led to the identification of at least 14 plant species eaten in the wild, with an additional 8 consumed by caged animals

Male red squirrel eating (*B. S. Turner*)

(Tittensor, 1970). In addition, the European red squirrel has been seen to eat sprouts, fruit blossom and even the berries of the yew tree, a species poisonous both to man and his cattle. Animal life is also eaten, and while much of this may be consumed incidentally during the course of herbivorous feeding, there is no doubt that animal protein does figure in the red squirrel's diet. There are records in Britain of the animal catching and eating fledglings and fully grown birds while, in Russia, S. I. Bozhko (1975) reports that passerine birds in Leningrad's many parks have difficulty in protecting their eggs from the red

56

squirrel. Siberian hunters are said to attract red squirrels to their traps with dried fish!

Such data give us a fair idea of the scope of the red squirrel's diet but not the proportions of the different foods. The red squirrel may indeed have extremely catholic taste but close observation has shown that, in the United Kingdom at least, the bulk of its nutriment is obtained from a single source—the seeds of several species of pine, especially the Scots pine, *Pinus sylvestris*. In Scotland, and in most other parts of the UK, this tree forms the greater part of the squirrel's diet. Food is first detected by smell (Frank, 1952) and is usually nibbled or tasted before being consumed or rejected. Nuts, and other attached foods such as pine cones, are gnawed free with the incisors and carried in the mouth to a suitable feeding site. The squirrel can hang upside-down to facilitate collection of the small light beech-nut. Red squirrels feed mainly in the canopy, and any food collected on the ground is normally taken up to a tree stump or large stone (Millais, 1905) for consumption, or it may be carried up the nearest tree and eaten there (Shorten, 1954.)

Once at its chosen site, the squirrel must extract and consume the edible part of its prize. The food is invariably held between the knuckles or palms of the forefeet (Barrett-Hamilton and Hinton, 1921), the clawed 'fingers' being used to rotate the food as required. There are two feeding positions: the squirrel may squat on its haunches with the tail held over the back (an attitude known to every child from picture books), or it may take up a less familiar position, hanging head-

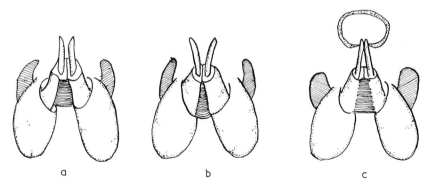

a   b   c

4. Squirrel jaw movements (a) at rest (b) open (c) closed to extract nut

downwards, secured to a support by the hind-feet. The squirrel's jaws are especially adapted for their job. By activating certain muscles, it can move the incisors of the lower jaw either towards (closed) or away from (open) each other (see fig 4). This peculiar jaw action is especially useful when dealing with hard-shelled nuts such as hazel. These are held by their larger end and a hole gnawed at the other. The lower incisors (closed) are then inserted and levered up, breaking off a portion of the rind. If the hole produced is large enough the kernel is extracted; if not, the incisors are again inserted and the process repeated.

Pine cones, the staple food of the British red squirrel, require a different technique. The squirrel chooses a feeding position, usually close to the main trunk to avoid being blown off in high winds. It then collects cones for as long as possible from this position, without moving its hind-feet (Gewalt, 1975). When cones are no longer available, it moves out into the more flexible outer branches, following each shoot to the end in its search. When located (and judged edible) by the squirrel's nose, the cone is gnawed free and carried back to the original feeding position. With the cone held between its forefeet, the squirrel bites off each scale in turn, starting at the base. Each scale contains one winged pine seed, and these the squirrel licks from the cone and holds in its thumbs to eat (using its remaining fingers to keep the cone secure). Only the seeds are eaten, the seed-wings and finally the core of the cone are discarded. It is a noisy affair and the red squirrel can easily be detected from some distance away when feeding in this manner. If located, it will usually 'chuck' angrily at the intruder, sometimes with the cone held in its mouth or even while eating.

After taking cones from one tree the squirrel will move, via the canopy, into the next and the feeding process will recommence. Squirrels consume prodigious quantities of cones in this way. The Russian scientist Holzmaier (1948) reported that in Siberia one squirrel fed on 190 cones in a single day. Tittensor (1970) estimated a daily average of 115 cones per day at Edensmuir in Scotland, making a grand total of at least 40,000 cones each year for each squirrel in the forest! As each pine cone contains 50 pine seeds (a conservative estimate), a single squirrel is responsible for the consumption of a staggering 2 million seeds in the course of a year.

Red squirrel eating (*B. S. Turner*)

The Grey Squirrel's Diet

The favourite food of the grey squirrel is not the pine, but the oak. Most grey squirrels will eat acorns, if available, in preference to any other natural food. Even before the seeds are formed they will invade oak trees and consume the catkins. For secondary supplies, the grey squirrel feeds on similar foodstuffs to the red, though in what proportions is not known. As with red squirrels, the amount of animal food consumed is very small, vegetarian items forming the staple part of the diet. Pine seeds are taken, as are elm, hornbeam, sycamore, spruce and larch. Beechmast is also collected, though it is doubtful if the heavier grey squirrel can emulate the acrobatic skill of the red by hanging upside-down to collect it. Larger kernels, such as hazel, walnut and both types of chestnut, are also taken in season. A wide variety of woodland fruits are eaten in autumn and help the animal to lay down a thick layer of fat against the twin blights of winter: starvation and cold. From personal observation it seems likely that, after nuts, fungi figure prominently in the diet of the grey squirrel. Several (unconfirmed) reports mention the creature taking fungi onto branches to dry them out. Red squirrels certainly do this, placing fungi in tree clefts for storage (Harvie-Brown, 1880-1).

Both species attack the trunk of various trees, stripping the bark, and in many cases causing severe damage (see Chapter 9). They are probably seeking the plant's vascular tissue which consists of xylem and phloem, and forms the tree's plumbing system. The xylem transports water and mineral salts upwards, the phloem takes organic nutrients in the opposite direction. Both flow at high rates during spring and probably tree-barking enables the squirrel to take advantage of these nutrients. It is certain that sap, for whatever reason, is attractive to squirrels. Kjelsaas (1972) observed a red squirrel licking sap from at least three different gnawing sites in early spring.

The squirrel finds most of its food by smell. One animal, after being trained to tip up a glass tube containing a hazel nut, ignored the tube if a boiled pebble was inserted instead. But the same squirrel would seek and even attempt to eat the pebble if before the test it had been left for one hour in a pile of hazel husks (*Corylus* spp). Red squirrels can find

60

Burying

quite deeply buried nuts, but only if the weather is damp: in snow they can locate food at depths up to 300mm (12in). Weight also plays a part in nut selection. When given empty hazel nuts, the animal from the boiled-pebble experiment at first responded by opening them every time, but later in the test series empty nuts were handled as if the squirrel was weighing them, and were then discarded intact. Nuts weighted with lead were at first either buried or opened, confirming that the squirrel did use the weight of the nut in determining if it was 'good' or 'bad'.

Nut Hoarding

Squirrels are famous for their 'foresight' in storing nuts for the coming winter, burying them underground or hoarding them in tree-holes. Shorten (1954) describes several instances of such caching, including a hoard of beechmast found in an old woodpecker hole. Both red and grey squirrels make caches of nuts, but in each species the impetus for burying or storing is a surplus of food, not prescience about future weather conditions. If given enough food, squirrels can be made to store nuts in any season. However in nature the period of super-abundance, autumn, is followed by a dearth of food in winter. The squirrels' behaviour is therefore neatly slotted into the cycle of the seasons, greatly aiding its survival during this lean time. Experiments in Germany have shown just how stereotyped a behaviour the act of burying is.

When burying a nut the red squirrel's movements can be broken down into a five-step sequence: (1) scratching a hole with the forepaws; (2) depositing the nut; (3) tamping the nut down with the snout by a series of rapid blows; (4) covering the nut with earth using a 'sweeping' movement of the forepaws; (5) packing the earth down by alternate stamping with the front paws (fig 5). But just how much of this complex sequence does the squirrel learn from its parents or older squirrels, and how much is inborn? Ethologists (students of animal behaviour) use so-called 'deprivation experiments' to answer this question. The scientist denies the animal any chance of practising the behaviour under study until it has reached a certain age. He then places it in a situation which usually elicits that behaviour in a non-deprived animal, and watches its reactions.

Iranaeus Eibl-Eibesfeldt (1967) took 18 young squirrels from the nest before they had even opened their eyes and denied them the oppor-

5. Squirrel burying nut (after Horwich, 1972)

Grey squirrel at hoard

tunity to dig or to handle any solid particles. When 5 of these animals were finally given nuts at 2-2½ months of age, they immediately went through the whole sequence of burying, from step (1) to step (5). The remaining 13 animals were given their nuts in a room without soil or 'diggable' material. Of these, 3 went through the whole (1) to (5) burying sequence; it was as if they were acting out an elaborate charade. They dug a non-existent hole in the hard flooring of the room, tamped it down, covered the nut with imaginary soil and finally patted the 'soil' down to make sure the nut was secure! Seven other squirrels performed the first three steps of the sequence before stopping, perhaps in puzzlement, while the 'brightest' three performed actions (2) and (3) only. In every case, when a squirrel 'buried' its nut it was attracted to the base of a vertical object, such as a chair-leg.

It seems, therefore, that given a normal upbringing and the correct situation, the red squirrel has very little to learn when it comes to burying. It has an innate skill which appears to be programmed or 'wired in' to its brain, and which requires only the correct trigger to be run off as a co-ordinated whole. Ethologists call these programmes fixed action patterns (*Erbkoordinationen*, German) and the objects that release or unlock the programme (in this case a nut, and less importantly diggable material) are known as key stimuli. It is easy to see the evolutionary virtue of such a strategy: it allows a short-lived creature like the squirrel to accomplish complex actions without time-consuming trial and error or imitative learning.

In the forest the programme works well. Even if the squirrel has never seen a nut or even another of his kind performing the burying sequence, the sight (and probably the smell) of the nut triggers the burying programme. The animal seeks the base of a vertical object (in a forest this would invariably be a tree), and buries the nut. Later in the year, when food is scarce, its acute sense of smell will find it again. It all looks so cleverly thought-out. Only when the scientist moves in does the 'intelligent' squirrel appear more like an organic robot, diligently expediting its programme even in completely unsuitable surroundings. I am not sure I was not happier with my illusions!

Tree Houses

With food supply taken care of, the squirrel's main priority is a place of refuge, a 'home' in which it can avoid the worst vagaries of the weather. Most rodents are ground dwellers with nest-holes dug into the soft soil of a field or river bank. Some eccentric squirrels have tried ground nesting: red-squirrel nests have, for example, been found in hollow felled trees, under reeds covered with snow, in a gorse bush and in a church tower (Barrett-Hamilton and Hinton, 1921; Ognev, 1940); grey squirrels occasionally nest among plant stems (the bilberry,

Vaccinium myrtillis), in corn stacks or rabbit burrows, under tree roots and in the roofs of various buildings (Middleton, 1931; Shorten, 1962a; Tittensor, 1970). But most squirrels keep to trees; and this poses a problem. Trees are exposed places in which to live. They are not very stable structures and wind speeds increase the higher one rises from the shelter of the ground. One answer would be to get inside the main trunk of the tree, but even with their specialised incisors squirrels would be hard put to cut a livable-sized hole in any tree. They do sometimes enlarge a hole formed when a large side branch was lost by wind-snap and the wound hollowed out by wood rot, but such natural holes are not abundant, especially for the red squirrel in conifer plantations. The family Sciuridae solved this problem a long time ago by emulating the birds and building a nest in the branches. But they improved on the designs of most birds by giving their nest a waterproof roof. The nest, usually referred to as a drey (or jug), is a spherical structure about 240/350mm (9-14in) in diameter and made of two main layers: an outer husk of branches and a central core of warmer, more insulating material (fig 6).

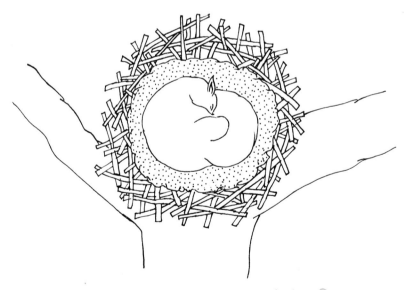

6. Diagrammatic cross-section of a drey

In Russia, Ognev (1940) described the red squirrel's construction of temporary summer nests (sometimes cup-shaped like a bird's nest) used for resting during the hottest part of the day. The British red squirrel does not build these, so they are probably an adaptation to the more extreme temperatures of continental Russia. Grey squirrels are also thought to construct summer nests, though once again not in the British Isles. The outer framework of a normal drey is invariably composed of branches taken from the tree where it is built. This leads to differences in the appearance of grey and red squirrels' nests: the grey's nest, composed of broad-leaved twigs which do not easily lose their leaves, is best described as an amorphous mass of brown foliage, whereas the red squirrel's (coniferous) drey, being leafless, clearly shows the spherical shape and intricate interweaving of branches and twigs.

Tittensor (1970b) made a detailed study of 12 such red-squirrel dreys from Edensmuir in Scotland. He divided the nest into outer frame and lining, and weighed each separately, as well as measuring the external diameter. The results, shown in Appendix 3, revealed a broad variation in total weight (from 195 to 638g, 7-22.5oz), mainly due to differences in the weight of the outer frame, whereas the weight of the lining remained fairly constant. The outer frame was invariably composed of pine branches, and older dreys had been refurbished from time to time with fresh twigs. The lining was composed of whatever soft material was to hand. Most were of grass and moss, but others contained varying amounts of feather and fur; a single drey contained large amounts of cotton-like plumes: seed-heads from the rosebay willow herb (*Epilobium angustifolium*). Other items used were deciduous leaves, shredded bark and lichens.

The drey is a very conspicuous sign of a squirrel's presence, especially of the grey which constructs a larger drey sometimes high in the tree canopy. This species will nest in many different types of tree, but as already indicated usually in deciduous varieties. The red squirrel obviously prefers conifers (larch and pine are favourites) and a more sheltered position close to the main trunk of the tree, either in the trunk itself or where the trunk makes an angle with a large side branch. Dreys can be erected on the site of an old bird's nest, or a disused drey, but most are contructed in a new site each year. There seems to be a definite height limit; Tittensor found no nest below 3m (10ft), and almost 90 per cent of the 97 dreys he studied were at 8m (26ft) or higher in the canopy. One was at 18m (59ft). Other authors agree broadly with these figures. Ognev (1940) gives drey heights of 3·3 to 20m (11 to 65ft), Raspopov and Isakov (1935) 4·8 to 14·8m (16-49ft), and Shorten (1962a) 3·6 to 18·2m (12 to 60ft). The grey squirrel has a similar range. According to Brown and Twigg (1965) this species builds, on average, halfway up any tree it settles in.

The drey helps the squirrel in several ways. It acts as an efficient shelter from inclement weather, and especially as an insulator against low temperatures. Work in Russia (Raspopov and Isakov, 1935) has shown that the temperature inside an occupied drey is several degrees warmer than the external temperature. It provides accommodation for the female to bear and rear her young, and for both sexes to sleep overnight. It may also protect against predators, especially raptors such as the sparrowhawk, goshawk and kestrel, although it is doubtful if the nest would be adequate protection against a determined wild cat or pinemarten.

As with humans, the ownership of a home in a desirable area where food is plentiful means that the squirrel has 'arrived'. It can now look for a mate and begin the process of raising young. How the squirrel does this, how it wins its own piece of territory, and how it relates to the other squirrels in its area, are the subjects of our next chapter.

6
Behaviour, Territory and Mating

If we were to study Man as a zoologist studies other animals we would soon conclude that he is a species bound by certain seasonal constraints. In summer we would find the creature basking in deck chairs until late evening, migrating to the beaches or the countryside, there to indulge in seemingly pointless behaviours. But with the coming of winter, the species all but disappears from the outdoor world. It spends its time in warm, well-constructed nests, venturing into the external cold only when absolutely necessary. In this, *Homo sapiens* is no different from most other mammals of a temperate clime. The badger retires to his sett for longer and longer periods as the weather closes in; mice and rats leave the fields for the warmth of barn and farmhouse; bats and dormice hibernate.

The squirrel, contrary to popular opinion, does not hibernate; both our resident species can be found out and about on the coldest days. However, the squirrel is not by any means oblivious to the quirks of our weather. As with most humans, in high winds, cloud, rain, mist, fog and snow the squirrel will stay at home for as long as possible. The food situation, too, may influence activity. For example, only a short day is required to collect sufficient beechmast for the squirrel's energy requirements. But when only pine cones are on offer, a much longer time is needed to extract an equivalent amount of energy, and the greater part of the day will be needed for foraging.

The activity cycles of grey and red squirrel are arguably the best-known aspects of their behaviour; certainly countless man-hours have been spent amassing data on them, Because of its importance in the United States' shooting calendar, American studies of *S. carolinensis* have been the most detailed work to date. The information derived

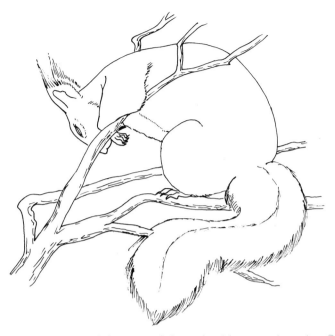

7. Red squirrel sleeping while wedged between branches

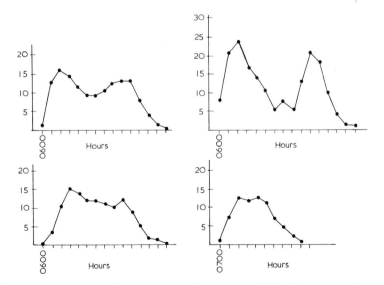

8. Activity patterns of a grey squirrel population (after Thompson, 1977)

69

from such studies agrees broadly with that found in both English species, so it will be instructive to follow the behaviour of the American squirrel in some detail.

Activity Round the Year

It is most active during summer, and least go-getting during winter, with autumn and spring bringing intermediate activity levels. A typical summer's day begins around first light; the animals emerge from their dreys, stretch, groom, perhaps yawn, and are then ready to begin the day. Activity increases rapidly, rising over the space of two hours to a morning peak. During this time, the squirrel is foraging (either in the canopy or on the ground), interacting with its fellows and occasionally resting briefly.

As the morning wears on, movement declines steadily until it reaches a minimum between 12 noon and 2 pm. The squirrels spend most of their time resting during this two-hour break, either retiring to their dreys or dozing while wedged between forks in the branches. (fig 7). Then a second increase in activity mimics the first in intensity and duration, after which the squirrel's activity steadily decreases until it returns to the drey to sleep sometime around dusk.

When displayed graphically, this pattern of activity results in a two-peaked, or bimodal, profile (see fig 8), which agrees well with that described by Ognev (1940) for the red squirrel in Russia. Ognev mentions a midday rest period and two activity peaks, one in the morning and the other in the afternoon, with the squirrels foraging and resting alternatively. Shorten (1954) and Shorten and Courtier (1955) have described a trimodal (three-peak) summer activity profile for both the red and grey squirrel in England, the third peak occurring during the midday period. However, Thompson (1977) considers such observations do not accurately mirror the actual activity pattern, at least for the grey squirrel.

All agree, however, on the diurnal patterns for the rest of the year. In autumn and winter, the late arrival of the sun means that the squirrel's day also begins later. The intensity of activity is likewise depressed. In autumn there is still a slight bimodal appearance to the activity graph,

70

Red squirrel with nut—to be cached near the base of a tree (*Bjorn Huseby*)

but it is much less pronounced. As the day-length shortens, the time available for the squirrel's business becomes more and more compressed, so that the midday 'rest' period is gradually squeezed out. By mid-winter, the process is complete, the squirrel is active for a single period during the day, and the activity graph has a single peak.

The northern hemisphere begins to nod back towards the sun and by mid-spring the graph once more assumes a two-peaked shape. Intensity during these active periods, and rest during the noon trough both increase as spring wears into summer, and by the middle of July the graph has come full circle—the squirrels are back once more to their two-shift system with a noon 'lunch-break'.

With both red and grey squirrels, this summer pattern probably results from lying up during the hottest hours. Conversely, winter's single activity peak is due to a desire to use the hottest part of the day.

In the grey squirrel it has recently been discovered that the activity of male and female animals differs during the seasons. The female squirrel is more active during both spring and summer, probably because she requires more food as pregnancy proceeds and later when she is supplying up to eight young with milk. Both Thompson (1977) and Bakken (1959) have noted that the male squirrel is more active (or more easily trapped) during the winter period. The reason for this is not known, but it may have something to do with increased male territoriality during this period.

The Home Range

The social system of the squirrel is based upon two main factors: dominance, and the possession of a territory or home range. All squirrels living permanently in an area of woodland hold a definite home range which they inhabit for most of their lives. For the grey squirrel, the size of this area has been assessed most accurately by Thompson (1977). His figures, in hectares, for male and female squirrels over one year of age, are shown on the following page:

Grey squirrel drinking (*F. V. Blackburn*)

Sex	Summer (n)	Autumn (n)	Winter (n)	Spring (n)
Male	2.15 ± 0.2 (34)	2.2 ± 0.1 (22)	2.35 ± 0.45 (13)	3.95 ± 0.35 (12)
Female	1.4 ± 0.1 (29)	1.45 ± 0.1 (19)	1.5 ± 0.2 (17)	1.85 ± 0.2 (17)

Thus, on average, each male squirrel occupies just over 2ha of land and each female around 1½ha. The figures for red squirrel are slightly smaller, but the male:female difference is again present. Each territory is fairly stable except for an increase in both male and female home ranges during the spring.

In some animals (eg the robin, *Erithacus rubecula*), the home range is jealously defended from 'conspecifics', other members of the same species. This helps to spread members of that species evenly throughout a suitable area so that a habitat may be exploited more efficiently. While it is not a particularly social rodent (if compared, for example, with the prairie dog), the tree squirrel is by no means as anti-social as the robin. It uses another strategy to maximise its exploitation of such limited resources as space and food: it shares some of its land with a number of neighbours.

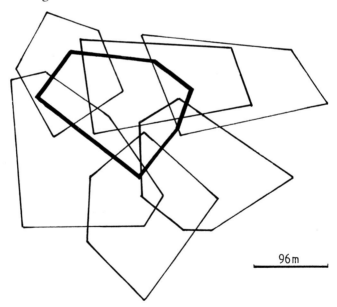

96 m

9. Overlap of the total home range of a selected squirrel (after Thompson, 1977)

The home ranges of all resident animals overlap extensively to form an interwoven system of territories. This can best be shown by taking a single squirrel's home range (the heavy black line of fig 9) and plotting over it the territories of all other squirrels which overlap it. Any squirrel in a given area can be selected for this example; the territory of each is partially overlain, as in the figure.

Marking Sites

With grey squirrels, the resident animals seem to choose certain trees as 'marking sites', stripping bark from the undersides of large branches near the ground and from the exposed areas of large roots. Urine and faeces are deposited here, together with secretions from the scent glands. To scent-mark correctly on the under-surface of branches, the grey squirrel has to project a jet of urine at right-angles to its body.

These marking sites act as notice-boards for the squirrel community and serve several different purposes. Simply by being there the marking site acts as a scent and sight 'warning', telling any non-resident squirrel passing through the area that the woodland is already occupied. In this case, the message is presumably 'move on'.

On the other hand, visiting males in the breeding season make a point of visiting the marking sites and sniff and clamber over them. This behaviour makes sense when the resident females' behaviour is taken into account. The females spend up to five minutes on a marking site (far longer than the males), sniffing, gnawing chips of wood from the tree, and wiping the marking point with scent from glands in the angulus oris (Taylor, 1968, 1977). As they leave they often squirt the site with urine.

It seems, then, that the females use the marking sites to tell the males when they are approaching, or in, breeding condition. Males from other areas visit the marking site to discover if it is worth remaining in the area for breeding or whether they should try their luck elsewhere. It is also possible that males, especially high-ranking males, use the site themselves to advertise that they are in the area. Recent evidence (Taylor 1977) has confirmed these theories. The times of maximum scent-marking and bark-stripping coincide with just those seasons

(May-June and August-September) when most immigrant squirrels are around.

Rank and Communication

If one divides the home ranges of squirrels by age or sex groups, there is no sign that either red or grey squirrels segregate themselves into, for example, exclusively adult male or exclusively juvenile female groups. In this respect, the squirrel lives in a classless society, each resident animal living as an individual in contact with squirrels of different ages and the other sex. This presumably facilitates social interactions while at the same time allowing the squirrel full use of the whole of its territory, for it will feed in all parts of its range. No squirrel restricts itself to, say, the southernmost part of its range, fearing it may meet a particularly hostile neighbour on its northern boundary. When feeding, it will cross the overlapping home-range boundary of any adjacent squirrel. As well as allowing each squirrel to make use of its whole territory, this 'non-aggression pact' between neighbours has the additional benefit of allowing 'clumped' feeding. If any food is locally abundant all squirrels whose home ranges overlap in that area will be allowed to feed.

How the squirrels recognise who is 'friend' and who 'stranger' is not yet known with certainty. Sight and smell are probably the most important senses involved, plus perhaps the occasional physical contact which each squirrel has with its neighbours. What is certain is that strangers are almost immediately identified, and just as quickly evicted.

Within an area of woodland each squirrel knows not only its neighbours but also its rank vis-à-vis each individual. Observations made at artificial feeding sites indicate that there is a well-defined 'pecking order' amongst both grey and red squirrels. All juveniles are inferior to all adults, and both sexes have a separate ranking system. These sexually defined ranks are not however completely separated; the dominant male squirrel takes precedence over all females regardless of their position in the female hierarchy, and the dominant females can only 'pull rank' on the most inferior of the adult males.

In the male system, and very probably in the female too, dominance is usually a function of age. The older the squirrel, the higher its place on the social ladder. Once established, such hierarchies lead to lowered levels of aggression between resident squirrels—only strange squirrels are attacked. These dominance relationships are established by aggressive encounters between squirrels. Chasing is probably one of the main determinants, the number of chases per unit time per month rising to a peak in late autumn and then falling to approximately one-eighth this value during July. Chasing avoids true fighting; one squirrel will usually concede to another by fleeing when chased by a more dominant animal.

But the chase is only the last in a series of less ostentatious challenge signals which the squirrel has at its disposal. Being a diurnal creature with the good eyesight necessary for tree climbing, squirrels do most of their communication—and they have a complex repertoire—visually, although other senses, such as scent and hearing, are also important.

The shape of any animal largely determines its range of visual signals. In the squirrel, the principal signalling organs are:

The eye: especially in the grey squirrel, where it is accentuated by lines of pale hair on the eyelids.
The ear: accentuated in the red squirrel by long pencils of hair, and in the grey by a puff of white hair behind.
The ventral surface: in contrast to the upper surface, the belly of both species is pure white, and stands out sharply when the animal sits up.
The tail: very important in both species, having long hairs which can be erected (using muscles in the tail) to increase its apparent size. In the grey squirrel the tail is accentuated by a white border along its length.

In addition, the whole of the squirrel's body can be used to convey meaning. A squirrel walking deliberately and confidently towards another eloquently proclaims its dominance, just as creeping and crouching acknowledges a subservient position.

Nor does a squirrel's communication system only establish and advertise social status; other visual, auditory and scent signals warn of predators, inform about food, or tell other squirrels the breeding condition of the signaller. For example, the male grey squirrel's testes change in colour during the breeding season to a very prominent black.

77

A list of signals and signalling behaviours (together with their probable meaning) is very hard to compile because of the difficulty of interpreting the subtle exchanges taking place, sometimes at high speed. One such list, for the grey squirrel, appears in Appendix 4. It is not exhaustive, but it does cover the more important signals which can easily be seen by any competent observer and tells us a great deal about the squirrel's way of life. When we total the number of signals for each function, we find that by far the greatest number, 21, are for dominance or submission, with those warning of danger or referring to breeding following at (9 and 7 respectively). The remaining functions have 1 to 4 signals each, defensive actions being the next most important.

Danger signals are essential for a small herbivore with very little means of active defence and whose best means of safety lies in concealment or flight. Reproduction, to maintain the squirrel population in the face of continual predation, is equally important, and it is no surprise to find a large number of signals subserving breeding. But what is surprising is the exceptionally high number of dominance/submission signals. Given the hierarchical nature of grey-squirrel society, a fair number of signals may be expected, but 21 does seem to be over-doing it, if all they are used for is territorial disputes. The answer seems to be that dominance interactions are not only necessary for the establishment and continuation of a territory, but vital in the important business of mating.

Breeding Behaviour

In the British Isles, both the red and grey squirrel have two breeding seasons: one in winter (January–March), the other in mid-summer (June–early August). Breeding is by no means automatic—several environmental factors can upset the internal workings of the squirrel's body, and either delay the breeding season or prevent it entirely. Failure of the food supply during or just after the food-critical winter period is the most common reason for breeding failure during January–March (Allen, 1943; Sharp, 1959; Smith and Barkalow, 1967), but this is far from the whole story.

A famous study by Nixon and McClain (1969) revealed yet another reason. A late spring frost markedly reduced the food supply of a group of squirrels which the scientists were studying, though the shortfall in provisions was not in itself serious enough to produce a reduction in breeding success. Nevertheless, during the following summer the squirrels 'skipped' a mating season, and the population fell dramatically. The two biologists could not understand why breeding had been abandoned until they realised that, prior to the frost, the squirrel population had been very large, close to the limit that the woodland could naturally support. After the frost, the smaller amount of food available caused much more competition between squirrels for this limited resource, and the amount of fighting and other forms of intra-specific competition increased.

'Social stress' is known to inhibit reproduction in a wide range of rodents (Christian, 1963), and the squirrels in Nixon and McClain's study had responded in classic style by simply refusing to breed. This shows how finely tuned the squirrel's responses are to the world about it in that, if conditions are such that their chances of survival are virtually nil, there is little point in bringing young squirrels into the world.

According to Shorten, it is the female squirrel who 'decides' when the breeding season shall begin. There are always some male squirrels in breeding condition no matter what the time of the year (Pudney, 1976), but the females come 'on heat' only once every twelve months, some in winter, the remainder in summer. In common with most rodents, male and female do not pair for life, or even for a season. The sexes consort for only a few hours during the breeding period, after which they go their separate ways. Courtship is likewise a brief affair. Only as the female approaches oestrus do the males in the population begin to take an active interest in their prospective brides.

Observable sexual behaviour begins with sexual trailing. The male, responding to olfactory cues from the female, follows a scent trail until he is within a few feet of her. She actively avoids him (Thompson, 1977), rarely allowing an approach closer than 1m (3ft). If he attempts to come closer she will either counter passively by moving away, or more actively with defence attacks such as lunging, pawing or tooth-chattering (Horwich, 1972) which decrease in intensity as the female

79

Red squirrel in hole (*Uno Berggren, Ardea Photographics*)

nears oestrus. Eventually, when the male approaches, the female allows him to sniff her vaginal region. He does this by stretching out his head and thrusting his nose under her outstretched tail. The female moves off, and the male follows, sniffing and licking as she progresses along the branches. In the early stages trailing often ends when, after following for several metres, the male seemingly loses interest in the female and simply wanders away. At any one time no more than one male is involved in sexual trailing, although the same female may be followed by different males at different times of the day. The inhibition to close approach of one male to another seems to prevent an aggregation of males during this early phase of mating behaviour.

Sexual trailing becomes more intense as the female approaches oestrus; she becomes more and more attractive to the males in the area and this leads to a breakdown in the taboo against male-male contact. Male squirrels from other species may even try to pay court to a female congener (Moore, 1968). As more males attempt to approach the female, the increase in aggression between the males in turn leads to greater agitation in the female who finally bounds away.

This change in the female's behaviour acts as a signal to the males, who begin to pursue the female while at the same time giving voice to a series of stifled sneezes (Bakken, 1959). This call is heard only during the mating chase and indicates that pursuit of a receptive female is taking place. Human observers can hear the 'sneezing' from a distance of at least 40m (120ft), and male squirrels can probably locate it from an even greater distance. Males seen running towards a mating chase frequently stop and assume an erect 'alert' posture, apparently listening, before they hurry on. The sound must be an effective lure, for up to thirty males have been observed pursuing a single female, most of them attracted by the 'stifled-sneeze' call. The progressive addition of chasing suitors results in increased activity in both female and males, leading to a heightened level of arousal in both sexes.

At times during the chase the female appears genuinely frightened, and may take refuge in a nest-hole or drey (Horwich, 1972; Barkalow and Soots, 1965) producing a pause in the chase. The female emits a 'hiccough-moan' during this time, after which she peers cautiously out of the nest. The dominant male of the pursuing skein of squirrels takes up a position as near as possible to the entrance and gives voice to a high-pitched alarm call. He may try to enter the drey but most of his time is taken up with chasing other subordinate males who continually approach the female's refuge. Aggressive encounters occurring both during the pursuit of the female and when she pauses in a bolt-hole help to sort out the dominance hierarchy of the chase. Thompson (1977) believes that the males become clumped into groups of approximately equal status, with the eldest males comprising the most dominant group. Following on from his foot-stamping and stereotyped tail-waving (fig 10), the aggressive chases between the most dominant male and his sub-ordinates are very fast and very vicious. Sometimes the dominant male succeeds in entering the female's sanctuary. Copulation may then

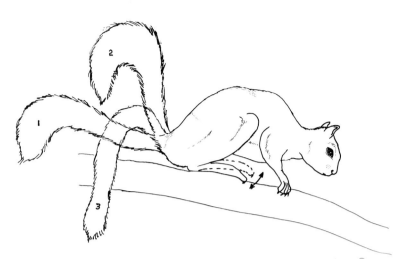

10. Male tail-waving and foot-stamping during mating chase ♂

♀   ←   ♂

11. Mating chase; hesitant approach to female by male ♂

take place inside the drey or nest-hole, but more often this pause in the mating chase ends with the female bursting from her hiding place and again fleeing the assembled males, who once again string out in pursuit with the most dominant animals in the lead.

A second type of pause occurs when the female, unable to find a drey or nest-hole, turns and faces the leading squirrel from a crouched position. She growls at the slowly approaching lead male and may even jump out at him with her forepaws extended. But the male is

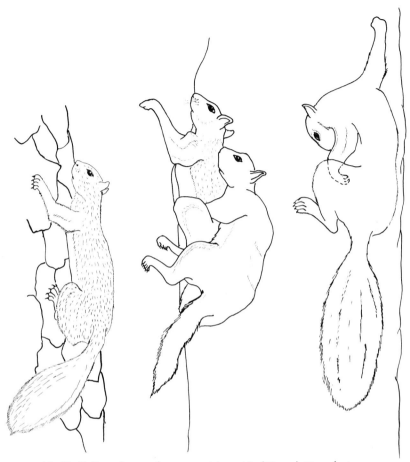

12. (*Left*) Female copulatory position; 13. (*Centre*) Copulation;
14. (*Right*) Male grooming genitalia

rarely discouraged by her lack of affection and continues his slow, hesitant approach. His tail hairs are always maximally spread and he may drape the tail to one side as a young squirrel does when approaching an unfamiliar object. This posture is very similar for a wide range of squirrel species; both the red (Eibl-Eibesfeldt, 1970), the grey (Horwich, 1972) and the North American tassel-eared squirrel, *Sciurus aberti*, indulging in these movements (Farrentinos, 1974).

83

In addition, the males of all three species call as they approach their intended mate, using sounds which seem to be a ritualised version of calls used between infant and mother.

This male strategy of infantile behaviour is found in many birds and mammals, and may serve to avoid the worst excesses of the female's violence. As the male closes with the female she will elude him by leaping over or around him, or by turning tail and running off. Pursuit and pause alternate until the female manages to out-distance the males by a sudden burst of speed and weaving. She then suddenly stops running and assumes the mating posture, usually on the vertical section of a tree (fig 12). The first male to reach the female is then allowed to mount immediately. Normally she clings to the bark with her forepaws, allowing the male to move the lower part of her body during copulation. In some cases the male may grasp the female's waist and pull her body backwards and upwards, in others her hindpaws rest fully under her rump in a non-extended position (fig 13), but in either event her tail is held to the side.

After copulation the female frees herself from the male's grasp and makes off. The male cleans and grooms his genitalia (fig 14) and then follows the female, driving off other males who attempt to approach her. There then follows a lengthy period (up to six hours) of post-coital chasing, in which the male pursues the female as in the pre-mating chase. There must however be an extremely rapid physiological response in the female, resulting in a change of scent or some other cue, for the male very soon loses interest in his former sweetheart. This is just as well, for as pregnancy proceeds the female becomes increasingly intolerant of any approaching male, even the previously successful suitor. Her whole being becomes intent on one thing only—finding a place of safety in which to give birth to her rapidly developing family.

7
Family Life

Almost as soon as the female becomes pregnant she undergoes a dramatic change in social status. Whereas before even the most dominant female was hard put to hold her own against the lower ranking males, she now becomes 'queen of the castle' at least in the domain of her own breeding tree. Here the female constructs the drey in which she will give birth to her young, or enlarges a previous one, lining it with soft material during a heightened phase of nest building. Around this time the grey squirrel mother-to-be becomes increasingly irritable and drives any male from the nest tree. Red-squirrel females are even more bellicose and often insist that the male remove himself not only from the nest tree but also from the general area in which it stands.

This war of the sexes is very common among rodents, and indeed in most major groups of vertebrates. It is part of the female's general aggressiveness towards all potential threats to her offspring. A breeding female, be she a turkey on her nest or a squirrel in her drey, is in a very exposed position. She must be ready to do battle with, and hopefully put to flight, a whole host of predators intent on securing a meal at the expense of her infants. Evolution has therefore decreed that as each foetus grows larger within her womb, her temper also increases. It is a brave male who will dare defy a breeding female squirrel; she is completely fearless during this period and will unhesitatingly attack any small creature that approaches too close.

Pregnancy lasts 38 days in the red squirrel, 44 in the grey. No one has ever seen a squirrel litter being born but the results—a bundle of baby squirrels—have been very thoroughly studied. In both species, development is very similar. The normal litter size is 5, though it may vary from 3 to 8, sometimes more, depending on the age of the mother,

Baby grey squirrel (*Ardea Photographics*) ?

the climate and the quality of food eaten during pregnancy.

The female squirrel is a model mother; she is very careful about the cleanliness of her brood and spends much time licking each infant individually while turning it in her forepaws. The young themselves look like small 76mm (3in) pieces of pink Plasticine and bear only passing resemblance to an adult squirrel. They weigh 11-15g (0·4-0·5oz) at birth (8-12g (0·3-0·4oz) in the red squirrel) and are blind during their first few days of life. The eyes are completely closed and show only a slight trace of a slit. The ears are bent forward, closed, and attached to the side of the head. There is no sign of teeth, and with the exception of short whiskers (1-2mm) on the snout, cheeks and ventral surface of the forearm, the young creature is completely devoid of hair.

Remnants of the dried umbilical cord, which before birth attached the infant to the mother, persist for the first three or four days after parturition.

Life and Growth in the Nest

The female grooms the young and suckles them at intervals from the four pairs of nipples which lie along the underside of her body. When suckling, the infant squirrel uses a 'pump-suck' action, its lips surrounding the base of the nipple and making it airtight. If separated from the teat during suckling, the babies will push forward in an attempt to make contact again. They do this by alternate movements of their fore and hind paws, but never with the adult four-foot sequence, which has not yet appeared. Their whiskers, the only hair on the naked bodies, aid in locating the nipple, for as soon as they touch the bare area around the female's teat, the infant will stop its forward motion and begin a side-to-side action of the head which brings its mouth to the nipple and milk. When they first begin to nurse, the young tread alternately with their forepaws (fig 15). This action begins on or around the fifth day, being most marked when there is competition between the young for suckling places (Horwich, 1972).

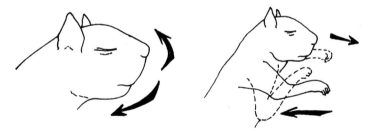

15. Nursing movements of infant squirrel

Even at this early age evolution has equipped the squirrel with several behaviours essential for its life in the nest drey. The infant lives literally on top of its brothers and sisters, and always attempts to move to the bottom of this sibling pile, where the warmth of the nest is at a maximum. It can scratch itself, though very ineffectually, roll from back to belly, and use its tail in attempts to stabilise itself when upset. Two other activities—squealing when disturbed and curling tightly into a ball when picked up—are especially useful as safeguards against predators. The squeal is used as a signal for help and often brings the female running to the infant's aid. Tittensor (1970) describes how a female red squirrel would approach quite closely when the juvenile squirrel he had trapped screamed in this way. The mother squirrel's approach would no doubt cause smaller predators to think twice before following through an attack, although it is doubtful if a creature such as the pine marten would be unduly worried by the female's courageous action. It's far more likely that he would regard her as a second helping!

If the mother squirrel judges that the breeding drey is too dangerous she will carry the nestlings one by one to a safer home. Unlike most animals the young are not lifted by the scruff of the neck but are carried with the mother's teeth gripping the loose skin of the limbs or flanks. In the red squirrel there is a remarkable skin fold running from the elbows to the flanks, reminiscent in many respects of the flight-skin of the flying squirrels described in Chapter 1. From birth onwards the young show a marked tendency to cling to any available object when picked up. So, when grasped on the flanks by the female, the infant squirrel holds on with its paws around one side of the mother's neck and wraps its tail around the other. Mother can then make off with this living bundle tucked safely beneath her chin.

Danger from predators is not the only stimulus to initiate litter movement. Nixon, Beal and Donohoe (1968) describe how one grey-squirrel female in Ohio, USA, moved her three nestlings 46m (150ft) from a damp, unhealthy nest to a tree cavity which gave good protection from inclement weather. Carrying distances of almost 152m (500ft) have been recorded (Shorten, 1954).

After two weeks the young have just a suggestion of hair along their backs, but they are still completely naked on belly and limbs. At three weeks the muzzle, head and tail are all quite well furred. Around this time too both eyes and ears open, and sight and sound begin to take a more important place in the infant's perception of the world around. The first teeth to show, the lower incisors, erupt from the gums be-

Grey squirrel albino—too conspicuous for safety (*E. T. Jones*)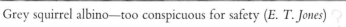

tween days 19 and 21 in the grey squirrel, and days 22 and 35 in the red.

As with physical appearance, the behaviour of the three-week-old squirrel becomes progressively more adult. Scratching becomes increasingly co-ordinated, with body stretching and tail stretching (both part of the adult squirrel's behavioural repertoire) also appearing around this time. Powers of movement improve in the nestling so that by day 20 the infant squirrel is able to raise its body and stand, supported only by its four legs. In the days following, fully adult walking emerges as the typical method of locomotion in quadrupedal mammals where, if the left foreleg is moved first, the right hindleg follows then the right foreleg and finally the left hindleg (Boulière, 1956). Once this behaviour is established the young begin feeble, unsuccessful attempts at climbing towards the top of the nest. By the end of the fourth week the infant squirrel has progressed far enough to manage a wobbly promenade around its nest, although loss of balance and occasional total collapse are by no means uncommon. During walking, the tail is held straight out or slightly raised, less often over the back in a typically adult manner. Growth continues during the fifth and sixth weeks by which time the whole body is covered with 1-2mm of hair, with 2-3mm on the tail. The lower incisors are now prominent and the upper incisors begin to erupt.

'Learning' to Keep Clean

'Learning' to keep itself clean predominates during this developmental stage: the adult urination posture emerges before day 40 (fig 16). The squirrel's body lies low on flexed hindlegs and is supported on the forelegs, to produce a squatting posture. The tail is sometimes deflected to the side. The infant squirrel begins to groom itself at around 30-40 days of age, and this is interesting in that every day or so the nestling 'learns' to groom a different part of its anatomy. The usual sequence (grooming of the hind limb, the rump, tail, genitals, arm and finally the foot) gradually emerges in that order. Strangely, washing of the face is the last to be mastered, as in many juvenile *Homo sapiens*. All these

Greys have the agility of a blue tit and are all too frequent visitors to bird-feeders (*Tom Leach*)

16. Urination posture ?

discrete washing actions are at first performed separately, but they gradually become co-ordinated into the complete washing/grooming/combing sequence of the adult. Anyone who has seen squirrels will be familiar with this rather stereotyped behaviour: the squirrel suddenly stops whatever it is doing on its haunches and commences its ablutions. However, the speed of its actions prevents one seeing what really happens; only by using slow-motion photography has the activity recently been analysed.

The squirrel begins with its head, closing the eyes and bringing its two paws simultaneously down over its nose, (fig 17). As the paws move off the nose the eyes open only to close again as the process is repeated several times, ending when the squirrel licks and grooms its paws and fingers. The forearm is groomed, then the face is cleaned once again, though this time the paws move just out of phase as they pass over the head. The eyes are closed and the ears held back during this action. The squirrel next turns its attention to its tail, working progressively from base to tip. While working on the tail its paws move out of phase and every so often it will stop to attack a particularly stubborn piece of pelage with its teeth. Next comes the left flank, after

17. Washing sequence

which the squirrel grooms and combs down the left leg to the foot. A third brush of the head follows, then the squirrel cleans its right side and hindlimb and finishes off with a quick scrub, if not behind the ears, at least very close to them. The whole cleaning programme, while requiring this paragraph of prose to describe, takes just over eight seconds.

The young begin to leave the nest during the seventh week, or very soon after. They are exceptionally 'cute' at this stage, still slightly unco-ordinated in their movements but looking exactly like miniature adults except for the head, which is proportionately larger in young animals and adds to their attractiveness in human eyes. Weight is around 110-130g (4-5oz) (Uhlig, 1955) about one-quarter the adult weight. About this time there is a change in the body-length:tail-length ratio, the tail growing rapidly until the the eighth or ninth week. Solitary and social play are now seen for the first time.

Play

Play is found to a greater or lesser degree in almost all mammals, especially before sexual maturity, but the reasons for it are still not completely understood. In most cases its movement or motor patterns are derived from ordinary activities which the adults of the species perform in their normal day-to-day existence, but in play these actions are usually executed in a repetitious, exaggerated or incomplete manner (Loizois, 1966). This has prompted some authorities to suggest that play is in some way a practice session in which the movements of adult life are perfected before they have to be used in earnest. Play-chasing (see page 96) seems to help a young animal to learn the best methods of escaping a pursuer, a skill that every squirrel certainly needs. But not all play is so obviously applicable to everyday life. When faced with a group of young otters taking 'turns each' on a mud-slide into a river, many a scientist will despair of ever discovering the purpose of play, and go off for a game of squash to let off steam. Which is, perhaps, just what the otters are doing.

In the grey squirrel solitary play consists of tumbling, acrobatics and creeping along or around an object, sometimes rubbing the body against this at the same time. This latter behaviour also occurs on the ground, when the squirrel rubs its ventral surface against a depression in the soil. A very common activity is play-fighting with an object: the squirrel lies on its back and manipulates for example a small twig between its four paws, frequently scratching and kicking it with the feet. The animal sometimes jumps and tumbles during the sequence.

My wife and I filmed such activity in adult squirrels, and found that adult object-play seemed to reach a peak during the breeding season. Presumably it is a way of releasing sexual energy which would otherwise remain 'dammed up' within the animal. This behaviour was interspersed with false flights, in which the squirrel would suddenly drop the play object and race away, zigzagging across the ground or scrambling up a tree for a short distance before returning to recommence object-play. For the red squirrel, Eibl-Eibesfeldt (1951) described similar object-oriented play, in which the squirrel takes the object in its forepaws, bites it and often kicks it with the feet. This last movement throws the object a few inches away; the animal immediately pounces on it and resumes the 'game'. Other species, eg the American red squirrel, *Tamiasciurus hudsonicus*, show similar solitary play (Ferron, 1975).

As they emerge from the close confines of the breeding drey, the young squirrels find infinitely more scope for exploration and social confrontation. So it is not surprising that between the seventh and tenth week all adult social behaviours (with the exception of breeding) become manifest. One important social activity is allo-grooming, when one squirrel grooms another. This behaviour is almost a compulsion—in the absence of other squirrels the animal will groom a variety of objects, including human fingers. It emerges between the forty-second and fifty-fifth day of life. One squirrel places its forefeet on the body of another squirrel, usually on the back. It then licks or bites the fur of the second animal with a short series of up and down movements, and ends this action by turning away the head and chewing or biting on the air. That the squirrel is actually eating something from the fur seems confirmed by the observation (Horwich, 1972) that a squirrel which groomed his fingers actually removed, chewed and consumed pieces of cuticle, skin and nail scrapings.

Although true sexual behaviour is not seen in squirrels of such an early age, its precursors become obvious during the seventh week. In general, this activity is initiated when a male grabs a female around the waist after leaping towards her in an unusual 'bouncy' gait. This bouncing apparently 'tells' the female that the other squirrel regards her as a playmate as opposed to a sexual mate. The female assumes an approximation of the copulatory posture, raising her rump, laying her tail over her back, and gripping the ground with her fore paws. The male then grooms the female briefly, leaps again into the air, regrasps her waist and repeats the procedure. If two males play this 'game' the mock-'female' will usually roll with his shoulder onto his back and then paw or kick at his playmate in order to get release.

Pawing is also used when the squirrel is on all fours and seems to act as a low-intensity defensive gesture, often seen when one squirrel attempts to take food from another. Pawing may be accompanied, as if for emphasis, by a whimpering growl.

In addition to sexual and defensive play, games of escape are very popular. Again, these frolicsome behaviours allow the juvenile animals to practise actions they will use in earnest during adult life. Eibl-Eibesfeldt has described how red squirrels practise escape manoeuvres by chasing one another. The chase itself seems to be the important part of the game:

> The pursuer is evidently much less interested in the situation than is the pursued. When the squirrels frolic in this way, each animal tries to hide out of sight of the other. If one squirrel sees its play partner coming, it rushes for cover on the other side of the tree trunk, waiting there to see if the partner will follow. The partner, however, 'thinks' that the movements of the other squirrel are directed against it, and so it too flees to the other side of the tree trunk; there the two squirrels meet, and each flees again. Thus, one can not distinguish in cases like this, which animal is pursuer and which animal is pursued.

Aggression or Submission

With such sophisticated social behaviour it is small wonder that things sometimes get out of hand and that peaceful activities become replaced by more pugnacious behaviour. Aggression is common to most vertebrate species, and so each has evolved a ritualised series of offensive and submissive postures and calls so that when it occurs no lasting harm is done to the protagonists. In the grey squirrel 'jumping at', chasing and aggressive grooming are all examples of such stereotyped behaviour which appear before the tenth week. In jumping at, the squirrel rears up on its hind limbs and reaches out towards its adversary with its forepaws. It pushes down simultaneously with both hind-feet and is projected towards the other animal. This may be sufficient to cow it; if not, one animal pursues the other at speed through the woodland. Growling and tooth-chattering by the dominant squirrel often follow a vigorous chase, possibly accompanied by rapid tail-flicking. A squirrel which finds itself outmatched has two main alternatives: it can either flee as far and as fast as it can from the aggressor, or it can attempt to appease its opponent by assuming a submissive posture, thereby indicating that it acknowledges the other's superiority and does not wish to contest the matter further. To appease an opponent, the animal usually takes up a stance which is the exact opposite of its formerly aggressive posture. Other animals do this also: when cocks spar, they hold their heads high, the bright red wattles of each bird acting like the proverbial red flag to a bull, angering its opponent so that both are ready for battle. But as soon as one cock knows itself beaten, it will put its head into a corner, thereby removing the temper-raising red flag from the sight of its opponent. When this happens, the fight ceases. In the squirrel, the appeasing gestures are also the antithesis of aggression. The squirrel holds its body as close to the ground as possible, and spreads its tail over its back with ears retracted.

The submissive posture, when held long enough, seems to inhibit a fully fledged attack from the aggressing animal. Often the attacking squirrel will not only cease to strike at its opponent, but will almost immediately begin to groom it. This grooming action is, however, very vigorous, almost vicious in its intensity, and seems to be a method by which the winning squirrel 'lets off steam' when prevented from launching a full-blooded attack. Similar aggressive grooming is seen in the jackdaw, when a beaten bird presents the nape of its neck to the victor (Lorenz, 1970).

Foraging and Feeding

Almost as soon as the young squirrels emerge from the nest they begin to forage in the adult manner, moving about with the nose very close to the ground while at the same time nodding the head up and down. The female never feeds the young outside the nest, leaving them to fend for themselves as best they can. If a youngster smells food it stops walking and begins rooting in the leaf litter or loose earth until the object of its interest is uncovered. When young, the squirrel is not quite sure which objects are edible and which should be ignored. As a result, it tends to stick close to mother and watch her as she eats. Captive

97

18. Juvenile variation of adult eating posture ?

squirrels can learn to open nuts more efficiently simply by watching a more experienced animal at work, and in the same way the young take their cue from their observations of mother. This does not stop them gnawing every object in sight however, including old bottle-tops and buttons. They are also inexpert when it comes to assuming the typical on-the-haunches eating posture of the adult. The youngsters seem almost inebriated as they attempt to balance in what for them is a terribly unstable position. For a few days they present an amusing spectacle as they first remain studiously erect, then begin to totter, and finally fall forward to end up resting on their forearms (fig 18). At about the same time (7 to 8 weeks of age) the young squirrels also stop eating food where they find it, and carry their booty to another spot for consumption. This again is very similar to adult feeding behaviour, and when combined with climbing leads the squirrel to consume its food in areas which possess a better field of view and are therefore safer. About ten days after the appearance of moving-before-eating the young have sufficient co-ordination and balance to eat while hanging by their hind legs (Horwich, 1972).

With the emergence of adult foraging and feeding the young squirrel is as prepared as it ever will be to face the many dangers of its environment alone. The time of protection and care is over; it must now take its place in the squirrel community, establish a territory and, hopefully, escape the many attempts on its life from a variety of diseases and predators.

8
Migration, Population and Disease

On leaving the breeding nest the young squirrels have a decision to make: they can either stay put and try to set up home in a small territory close to the nest-tree, or they can migrate out of the neighbourhood and seek their fortunes in pastures new. Recent research has shown that only a few squirrels—not more than one in ten—plump for the second alternative. This is not really surprising; most mammals are happiest in a region well-known to them, and will do all they can to remain within it. Long exposure to the same area allows a creature to discover and utilise all the many potential escape routes, so lessening its chances of falling victim to predators. A squirrel on the move in unfamiliar territory is far more vulnerable to attack than when it is on its own home ground; it has no idea which trees offer good avenues of retreat, and which lead, literally, to a dead end. It is much more easily disposed of by even its most ineffectual predator.

Such, indeed, is the fate of the vast majority of squirrels who think the nuts are sweeter on the other side of the valley. Even if they survive the attentions of stoat or fox there is no guarantee that their wanderings will take them into lands flowing with the squirrel equivalent of milk and honey. And if they do, there is a very good chance that they will find it already inhabited by members of their own species who, as we have seen in Chapter 6, are extremely intolerant of strangers and both ready and able to chase them from their territory.

Migrant squirrels are at a double disadvantage. They are young, which immediately sets them low in the dominance hierarchy, and not being on home ground, again decreases their status and makes them less likely to withstand an attack from a resident squirrel. Konrad Lorenz (1970) has shown how, in most cases, the animal in possession

Immature grey squirrel (*R. J. C. Blewitt, Ardea Photographics*) ?

of an area can successfully defend it from a newly introduced member of the same species. So it is small wonder that in every study so far conducted, very few if any of the migrant squirrels were able to secure a territory in an already established population. This is especially true in America where the grey squirrel has already expanded into all available habitats.

The migrants range widely and erratically once they have left the nest-site (there is no evidence that related animals move in the same direction), finding all available space colonised and pursued to the borders of the territory by every squirrel fortunate enough to hold a piece of land. In many ways their plight is similar to that of human paupers of the eighteenth century. These unfortunates were liable to

100

become the responsibility of the parish in which they happened to be living, and as no area wanted the expense of feeding them, they were constantly chased away over the parish boundary, only to find the same treatment waiting for them as soon as they entered the next parish. As an occupying squirrel's territory will overlap with several others (see page 74), as soon as the migrant has been chased to a border he finds himself attacked by the neighbouring squirrel. So the unfortunate creature is driven from every desirable area, constantly on the move until it either starves to death or is eaten by predators.

Migrants in the British Isles, especially greys, stand a better chance of survival than those in North America. In the United Kingdom there are still choice areas containing good nest-trees and an ample food supply so far unclaimed or where the population is at so low a density that a migrant can still find a small area in which to put down its roots. In the USA and Canada the number of 'pioneers' who find a home is very small indeed; every habitable plot is already occupied and jealously guarded. Only in Britain does the apparently cruel behaviour of the resident squirrels to migrants of their own species begin to make evolutionary sense. By chasing migrating animals from already colonised areas the residents force the travellers to wander over land previously unexplored by their species. A pair of squirrels may turn up more than forty miles from the nearest squirrel colony and, if they are fortunate and the area can support them, they will begin drey building.

The behaviour of such an isolated pair will not be very different from that of squirrels with neighbours of their own species, although they will obviously not be so preoccupied with 'status' as their more crowded brethren. Given a good food supply the pair will breed, the male enjoying unhampered access to his female, and the mating chase possessing none of the angry aggressive inter-male competition. If all goes well the new colony will expand; the original pair may mate regularly, or the female may accept her own male infants as consorts and the male may copulate with his 'daughters'.

Once the population has increased to a limiting level, the migration process will be repeated, more migrants moving out from this squirrel island in the hope of lighting upon an equally hospitable area which they in turn can colonise. But this situation is a temporary one; as soon as colonisation of all available habitats is achieved (and in the British Isles this can be a matter of at most another 100 years), any squirrel that prefers to migrate from the area in which it was reared will almost certainly suffer the same fate as its North American brethren.

Mass Movements

Other squirrel migrations are much more dramatic, and involve not just those animals seeking a territory, but the territory-holders themselves. The reason for such mass migrations is a simple one—lack of food. What normally happens is that a series of good seasons has led to the squirrels increasing, so that the population has reached, or is close to, the carrying capacity of the environment. Then in autumn when all the young of the year have been weaned, and when the population is therefore at its highest point in the annual cycle, disaster strikes: the main crop is small, or it fails entirely. At a stroke there is insufficient food for the squirrel population. So all the squirrels in the area move off in search of food, and a mass migration has begun.

Once started, such movements are almost impossible to stop. The travelling animals move into a second squirrel area, and because the migrants' numbers are so large, the residents find it impossible to drive them from their territory. The increased feeding pressure, with joining residents, soon strips the area bare of food. Then the squirrels of the second area also 'break camp' and join the migration. This tragedy is acted out again and again, and the squirrels swell in numbers from a score, to a regiment, to an army, to a huge uncontrollable horde. The greater the numbers, the less chance that any area will have sufficient food to supply their needs and so stop the migration.

In Russia, Kiris (1941) and Formosof (1933) have described enormous migrations of red squirrel. Rivers are no barrier to these hordes. Mighty torrents such as the Amur, Ob and Yenesi are attempted; and thousands of squirrels have perished when trying to cross the Tatar Strait, Lake Baikal or the Gulf of Finland. The grey squirrel has also been indulging in travels of heroic dimensions since at least 1796.

The squirrels move in a long 'skirmishing line', sometimes more than thirty-five miles in extent. The species is said by Shorten (1954) to be chary of water more than a mile or so wide, although in 1848 'two acres' of grey and black squirrel swam a distance of five miles in their crossing of Seneca Lake in New York state. As with the red squirrel, once the migration has commenced it proves virtually unstoppable, although its speed will not exceed 1-1½ miles each day. The squirrels may even pursue their route through human settlements. Several reports describe the damage done to agriculture during these marches, of corn fields denuded by hundreds of feeding squirrels, despite the presence of scores of people who were killing the invading rodents as fast as they were able.

Man is not the only creature interested in destroying squirrels. Wherever these long migrations occur, predators of all shapes and sizes swoop in from miles around to avail themselves of the easy pickings. Those squirrels that survive the gauntlet of such hunters find no respite. There is no chance of any area having sufficient food to satisfy the squirrel multitude, so the majority of survivors, pushing on slowly across the countryside, are inevitably condemned to a lingering death from starvation. If by chance the migrators run out of land and find themselves faced with an expanse of water, they will often plunge boldly in. Those American squirrels that swam the five-mile stretch across Seneca Lake could not possibly have *known* that there was land within their reach on the other shore. Had the waters of the lake proved to be an ocean, they would simply have swum on until their fur became waterlogged and exhaustion set in. Then, one by one, they would have drowned.

So far, in the British Isles squirrel movements have been more modest, though still sufficiently anomalous to excite more than local interest. Shorten (1954) reports that in October 1942 hundreds of grey squirrels were sighted by a Major Portal, travelling down the forest rides at Swanmore, near Southampton. The migration continued throughout the morning, the squirrels hurrying by without pause for rest or feeding. Presumably a bad nut harvest had impelled them to seek their food elsewhere. Five years later, again during October, a similar migration of groups of squirrel was observed. In the very early morning a lorry driver reported seeing approximately twenty squirrels approaching across a grass field (this in itself is unusual, squirrels almost never leave cover for the danger of an open field). The squirrels crossed the road and entered a small copse. In the same month, almost thirty greys were seen travelling in Indian file down a rut, so close together that only a single shot was required to dispose of five animals!

Migrating squirrels, whether travelling alone or in huge numbers, are always in the gravest danger. But those squirrels which stay at home also have their problems. The young first appear at the base of the nest-tree at around 9 to 10 weeks of age (Bakken, 1959; Thompson, 1977). If they decide to settle close to the tree, they try to hold a small area of land and slowly to increase the size of this 'bridgehead'. Horwich (1972) says that the maximum home-range expansion for a litter is reached at about 170 days, although another study (Thompson's, 1977) has shown that the majority of this home-range increase is achieved between 90 and 128 days of age. The females of a litter expand into most of the territory they will hold as adults before the males. This is because the females become sexually mature at least three months before their male siblings, and can therefore breed earlier and integrate more easily into the adult squirrel community.

Population and Disease

Along with the rabbit and the mouse, the squirrel is famous (or perhaps infamous) for its powers of procreation, but unlike the former two its reputation is not altogether deserved. The harvest mouse *Micromys minutus*, for example, breeds six or seven times a year in favourable conditions, has a litter of up to 11, and the young become sexually mature at 5 weeks of age (Harris, 1978). If all the progeny of one pair of harvest mice survived the year and bred at maximum capacity, by the end of the year there would be over 1,000 harvest mice. One begins to wonder why we are not wading through a brown sea of *M. minutus*! The answer is, of course, that most of the harvest-mouse population is destroyed in the first few weeks of life by a variety of predators including crows, foxes, stoats and even the humble toad. Only a small percentage live more than the first six months, though this is still sufficient to populate our fields with plenty of these charming creatures.

By contrast, both the red and grey squirrel breed at most twice a year and the average litter is, by harvest-mouse standards, paltry, being a mere five for both species. Even so, if unchecked this relatively low birth rate would still be too great. During normal years the squirrel population, as we have seen (page 74), is stable at around 1 animal per 4 acres for the grey squirrel (Thompson, 1977) and 1 animal per 3 acres for red (Tittensor, 1970). At birth the male:female sex ratio is approximately one to one, but as time passes male mortality is higher (probably because the males are the more adventurous of the two sexes) and there is a slight excess of females by the time the animals come into breeding condition. If the average litter is 5 young, and 10 per cent of these juveniles migrate, this leaves $4\frac{1}{2}$ squirrels born each year to every adult female in the population. This average, while not high by rodent standards, is too high to be allowed to grow unchecked. If the population is to remain stable, there must be other factors at work constraining the rate of increase and preserving a balance.

As with most other animals including primitive man, there are six main constraints on population level: old age, lack of food, weather, disease, parasites and predators. Old age is hardly a problem— it is unlikely that any squirrel lives long enough to become senile. Long before this time, one of the remaining constraints will have carried the poor animal off to wherever squirrels go when they depart this life. Although captive red squirrels have lived as long as 9 years, and grey squirrels to 15 years, in the wild few individuals will survive more than 5 years.

Ageing, therefore, is not a killer in itself; what it does is to 'set the squirrel up' so that it is too slow to escape its predators, or too weak to withstand the ravages of climate and disease. There are several accounts of squirrels freezing to death in their nests during particularly bitter winters. Disease produces considerable mortality, especially when the population is high.

Mange or scab is the most common infection in this country. It is caused by a mite (*Sarcoptes* genus) burrowing into the skin, often striking first at the tip of the ears. A scab forms at the site of injury and the surrounding hair may begin to fall out. The mite's activities are obviously extremely irritating to the squirrel, who tears at the spot

105

with its sharp claws, enlarging the site of infection and producing open sores. The effect on the infected animal varies; some grow new hair and recover completely, while others die within two months of contracting the disease. Coccidiosis—a parasitic infection of the liver or intestinal tract by certain sporozoa—can also account for large numbers of squirrel, especially the red. Enteritis may likewise be a cause of death; Tittensor (1970) reports that a dead adult female discovered on Brownsea Island, Dorset, had suffered from this disease just prior to her death. Ljubimov (1935) described an infectious disease of red squirrels (haemorrhagic septicaemia) in the USSR, where squirrels, along with many other rodents, are considered important reservoirs of tularemia, a disease which they may transmit to man.

In the United States and Canada there is no serious endemic disease of the grey squirrel other than mange. Whether the coccidiosis which affects the grey in the British Isles was contracted from the native red is a matter of conjecture. Middleton (1932) believes that it was responsible for the outbreaks of disease known locally as 'black scour' which greatly affected the British grey-squirrel population during 1924 and 1930-1.

Squirrel Predators

Although serious when they occur, outbreaks of epidemic disease are not a continual drain on squirrel numbers. But predators are, reducing the squirrel population by ones and twos throughout the year. Probably the red squirrel is now bothered less by predators than at any time during its long sojourn in the British Isles. The introduction of pesticides such as DDT during the 1950s all but removed one group of predators, the birds of prey such as the goshawk and sparrowhawk. Before, these birds had missed no opportunity of seizing a foraging squirrel, as well as a great number of small birds. The pesticides were taken up by the small birds and, because a bird of prey ate scores of them each year, the poisons gradually became concentrated in its tissues. These heavy concentrations affected the shell of raptors' eggs,

Grey squirrel with bird-feeder (*Tom Leach*)

A grey squirrel is well camouflaged in winter sunshine (*Ray Kennedy*)

making them so thin and brittle that they broke before the chick inside was fully developed (Ratcliffe, 1970, 1972). Thus, indirectly, these chemicals virtually removed the first of the squirrel's three main types of predator.

Fortunately many of the more harmful pesticides have since been abandoned and the raptor population has recently shown an encouraging increase, especially now that egg collecting has been outlawed and increasing numbers of keepers realise that the hawk and falcon are not as harmful to the lands under their charge as was previously thought. British squirrels may before long find life more difficult, goshawk and sparrowhawk regaining their natural place as regulators of rodent numbers.

When attacked, it is a case of every squirrel for itself; other squirrels will not attempt to help the unfortunate victim. The squirrel attempts to thwart bird attacks by climbing the trunk of any nearby tree in spiral fashion, a manoeuvre its winged adversary cannot emulate.

The wild cat, the second main predator, has no such problem. Its climbing ability is phenomenal; it can follow squirrels high into the trees and into their drey nests. If cornered, the squirrel will put up a desperate defence. Although primarily designed for gnawing food, its incisors make good weapons, capable of inflicting a vicious, even fatal, bite. The hindlegs are also pressed into service, being brought up under the squirrel's belly and thrust suddenly out and downwards in an attempt to disembowel the foe. This can be an effective mode of defence with the smaller carnivores like the stoat and weasel, but with the wild cat it is no more than a pathetic attempt to starve off certain annihilation. In the past the wild cat was a serious predator, but for the last fifty years the numbers of this beautiful felid have steadily declined, and it can now be found only in very remote areas, principally the Highlands of Scotland.

If the red squirrel was fast enough it could always escape this miniature tiger by taking to the topmost branches of a tree, where the heavy-weight wild cat could not follow. But no such deliverance was possible from the pine marten (*Martes martes*), the third in our trio of primary predators. As agile as the squirrel itself, once a pine marten had the scent of a squirrel in its nostrils there was very little hope of survival.

(*Above*) European wild cat (*Ian & Lesley Bearmes, Ardea Photographics*); ?
(*below*) Pine marten (*Åke Lindau, Ardea Photographics*) ?

No amount of skilful footwork or acrobatic leaping could shake off pursuit. The squirrel's only ploy, and one used frequently when pursued by this implacable mustelid, was to lead the pine marten to the outermost branches of a high tree and then, as the marten closed with its seemingly helpless prey, to launch itself from the topmost twig into the air. Squirrels can survive falls from a considerable height with no apparent injury—pine martens cannot. Unable to follow, the marten had to retrace its steps along the branch and down the main trunk before again taking up the chase. This brief respite sometimes allowed the squirrel to escape. Fortunately for the squirrel (though less happily for the ecological well-being of the British Isles as a whole), pine martens have become increasingly rare in recent years. While they do take squirrels in those few regions they still inhabit, they are no longer a threat to the majority of British squirrels.

Both red and grey squirrel are hunted casually by a number of other British carnivores. Almost any predator—fox, stoat, weasel or polecat —will kill squirrels if chance forces a meeting and they are swift enough to prevent their quarry's escape. Feral and domestic cats are an additional hazard and as there are upwards of 5 million domestic cats in the UK these creatures must take a considerable toll of young and aged squirrels, especially the grey squirrel in urban surroundings. On those rare occasions when squirrels forage at night (Tittensor 1970), they may fall victim to the larger species of owl. It is even conceivable that swimming squirrels (during migrations) may fall foul of pike. But none of these casual predators (except perhaps the pike) stand much chance if the squirrel they stalk is a healthy adult.

Both red and grey squirrels possess several efficient means of signalling the presence of danger to others of their species. The grey squirrel gives a single, sharp snort or a 'chuck-chuck charee' call whenever it becomes aware of an uncertain, though probably harmful, presence. If it decides to flee, usually when the predator comes into sight, it rapidly flags its tail over its back while retreating, thereby silently signalling a warning to its neighbours. Fit and fully grown squirrels of both species are far too alert and agile to fall victim to an opportunistic attack, but juveniles are not. Playful and not half as worldly-wise as their older relatives, squirrels of around 6 or 7 weeks of age suffer most from carnivores and predatory birds. Such adult squirrels as are taken are usually the oldest animals, or those weakened by diseases such as mange or by parasites.

Squirrel Parasites

Most animals harbour at least one parasite, even hyper-hygienic man. Parasites live either on (the ectoparasite) or in (the endoparasite) another organism (the host), from which they derive most, if not all, of their food. Some parasites have extremely complicated life cycles which involve more than one host; the cestode, *Taenia echinococcus*, for example, is found as a larval form inside domestic animals and man, and as an adult in the dog. Usually parasites do not kill their host; after all they have a vested interest in keeping their food supply alive! A parasite which kills off its host is effectively committing suicide. This is especially true for endoparasites; they have no chance at all of hopping onto another animal of the same species should their first host give up the ghost. But most parasites do weaken the infected animal and, as with bacterial diseases, such infestation serves to tip the scales in the direction of death.

The squirrel harbours a number of external and internal parasitic organisms, all of which debilitate their host to a greater or lesser degree. In the United States, Davidson (1976) collected 270 grey squirrels from 18 localities and examined them for internal parasites. He found no less than 23 species of multicellular endoparasites: 2 trematodes, 4 cestodes, 1 acanthocephalian and 17 species of nematode worm! Seven of these parasite species had produced lesions in the organs of the host, indicating that the squirrel was being significantly harmed. In parts of the United States, for example eastern Texas, the larvae of the harvest mite can be the most damaging external parasite of the grey squirrel during summer months. The harvest mite also 'lunches' on the British grey squirrel, though to a less serious extent.

The characteristic flea of *S.carolinensis* is *Orchpaeas howardi*. The American grey is hardly ever without this uninvited guest and it is no surprise that *O.howardi* has also been introduced into the United Kingdom via its host. Six flea species from other animal forms have also been discovered lodging in grey-squirrel fur, the most common being the rabbit flea *Spilopsyllus cuniculi*. Presumably squirrels taste just as nice as rabbits!

At least three separate species of lice inhabit the grey squirrel's pelt: *Enderleinellus longiceps*, *Haplopleura sciuricola* and *Neohaematopinus sciurinus*.

Tapeworms, *Taenia taenioformis*, have been found in grey squirrels from North Carolina and Texas, while nematode worms *Longistrata hassli*, were discovered in 92 per cent of grey squirrels examined in North Carolina. In the United Kingdom nematode infestation seems less marked. Middleton (1931) found only slight infection by these parasites (5 per cent of total animals examined) in the introduced grey.

The red squirrel is no less plagued by parasites. Apart from the protozoons—which include the coccidiosis-inducing *Eimeria* genus—there are at least a dozen lice, ticks and other assorted 'nasties' which live on or inside *S.vulgaris*, including:

Lice:	*Enderleinellus nitzschi*
	Neohaematopinus sciuri
	Polyplax sphaerocephala
Ticks:	*Ixodes ricinus*
	Ixodes trianguliceps
Helminths:	*Enterobius sciuri*
	Trichostrongylus retentaeformis
	Oxyuris acutissima
	Oxyuris ungula
Siphonaptera:	*Monopsyllus sciurorum*
	Orchopaeas howardi
	Tarsopsylla octodecimdentata

(Shorten, 1954; Blackmore and Owen, 1968)

There is something inherently ugly about parasitism. The life-style of other creatures, the scavenging vulture for example, might seem abhorrent to human eyes, but at least one can see a reason—the disposal of carcases in the vulture's case—that justifies their existence. It is hard to find any redeeming feature in the parasite's way of life. Yet some people in Britain regard the parasites of squirrels with affection. For some, foresters in particular, it is a case of 'the more the merrier'. Their rationale is that squirrels are vermin, a pest to be destroyed by fair means or foul, and if parasites can help in this task, so much the better. Their reasons for believing this vary, but most hinge on the subject of our next chapter: whether the economy of a country is materially affected by the presence of the squirrel.

9
Friend or Foe?

Rodents have always been a thorn in the flesh of mankind. In Great Britain alone, it is estimated that the destruction caused by a single species of rodent, the brown rat, is worth more than £100 million per annum. Of all the rodents, the rat is the *bête noire*, causing not only monetary damage, but posing a serious danger to health, as does its more compact compatriot the mouse.

Rats and mice are economic damage writ large, but other rodents can be just as harmful. In the USSR, great efforts are made annually to prevent the increase of ground squirrels who consume crops and damage grasslands (Polyakov, 1959). These seed-eaters take vast quantities of freshly planted cereals such as rye, oats and barley, and remove and store grain from the growing plant long before it is ready for harvesting by man. The position was considered so serious by the Soviet authorities that poison grain was distributed over wide areas by truck, and even by aeroplane. Polyakov (1959) estimated that 150 million ground squirrels were destroyed annually by this method, and yet the species continued to thrive!

The huge numbers of rodents, especially in large continents, means that it is virtually impossible to get rid of any disease they may carry. If such diseases are transmittable to man, then wherever human and rodent populations overlap there is a very good chance of cross-species infection. Eating an infected animal or simply skinning its body is often sufficient to produce illness or even death. Because of their almost infinite numbers, the marmots of the central Asiatic plateau were an important ancient source of plague, transmitting the disease to other species of rodents and finally to humans. With the advent of regular sailing routes around the world, it was only a matter of time before other parts of the globe became infected. Rats from coastal towns, infected from alien ship-borne rodents, spread the disease to suburban species and thence far and wide across the country.

Sylvatic plague first reached the USA in 1900 by way of the seaport of San Francisco, and the plague bacillus was isolated from the Californian ground squirrel in 1904, making it evident that the disease had spread to the surrounding countryside in the space of 4 short years. It crossed the mountain barrier of the Sierra Nevada into Oregon and within 35 years had infected the rodents of 10 States. Between 1930 and 1939 as many as 8 cases of human infection with sylvatic plague were recorded, and there must have been many more; the disease was well-established among ground squirrels over a wide area making eradication impossible. The rodent then, is rarely the friend of man. At best, like the flying squirrel of south-east Asia, it is neutral, neither harming nor helping man's efforts to survive in what, at times, is an extremely hostile world.

Though certainly not harmless, squirrels fall somewhere in the middle of this classification. The sciurids *are* an economic liability in the United Kingdom and elsewhere, though not on the grand scale of the murids—the rats and mice. But the squirrel can sometimes be useful; let us look at the bright side first.

Squirrels for Beauty, for Sport—or Food

One point seldom considered in our finance-obsessed world is the squirrel's beauty. Probably few people are so zoologically insensitive as to be unaware of how aesthetically pleasing the squirrel is, especially our native red. With its cute elfin ways and anthropomorphic mannerisms, it appeals to even the most hard-hearted 'misozoologists'. It is hard to see how anyone can even dare to put a price on the joy of spying one of these red-furred elves of the tree-tops. Unbelievable as it is, the granite-faced world of politics and high finance seems to utterly ignore such aesthetic considerations, in the same way that the *raison d'être* of National Parks and other 'islands' of natural wilderness is often the amount of foreign currency they can attract. The powers-that-be seem to prefer to reduce everything to terms of dollars, so that the rationale for the continued existence of the red or grey squirrel must be that the beast is useful in the production of paint brushes, or that its fur is coveted by rich women from the more affluent nations. Yet it is a pound to a penny that such financial high-flyers take their vacation in some natural beauty spot, giving the lie to their artificial economics by recharging their batteries and calming their minds amidst the wonders of the natural world.

That the squirrel's good points outweigh the bad is especially true for those nations where the squirrel forms part of that select and unfortunate group of animals who provide 'good sport' for marksmen. Only the rabbit is more important as a game animal in North America, while in Finland squirrels are said to be the most important sport animal. In the United States there is even a closed season on the grey squirrel to allow its numbers to build up to high levels.

Since early times, the red squirrel's pelt has had commercial value. Barrett-Hamilton found reference to the export of Irish squirrel hides from around AD 1243. Other records tell of exports from England to Scotland, some of these hides having come from as far afield as Flanders and Russia. Russian red squirrel gives the best hides, the colder winters making for denser, and therefore more luxurious, pelts. The same is true for the Canadian grey, and squirrels from this region are famous for the quality of their fur. In America, the grey squirrel has always been regarded as a good fur-animal and even today fine mittens or foot-warmers are made from the skins of those animals shot for sport. Minor industries include the use of squirrel hair for paint brushes and for anglers' flies.

Some Americans have a stranger use for the grey squirrel—they eat it! In Britain during World War II, North American servicemen offered as much as 5s (25p) for a dead squirrel. The meat is said to taste very much like rabbit, and having twice eaten it I can vouch for its palatability, although the taste seems to me rather blander than wild rabbit. One has only to overcome one's preconceptions that squirrel, like dog or cat, is something that is not 'proper' food. For the more adventurous gourmets living in areas that have large squirrel populations, two recipes in which squirrel meat can be used are given on the following page.

117

Squirrel and Nut Galantine
Cut all the meat from 3 uncooked squirrels. Put the bones and giblets into a saucepan with 1 pint (500ml) of water. Season, cover the pan and simmer for 1 hour. Meanwhile, mince the squirrel meat, add to this 4oz (100g) chopped nuts (almonds are best but any type of nut will do), 2oz (50g) soft breadcrumbs, 2 eggs and a $\frac{1}{4}$ pint (125ml) of chicken stock. Season the mixture well and place in a well-greased loaf tin. Cover with greased foil, stand the container in a little cold water, and bake at 325-350°F (170-180°C: gas mark 3-4) for $1\frac{1}{2}$ hours. Cool in the tin and weight the top as the galantine cools; this makes it easier to cut.

Squirrel and Vegetable Stew
Cut the flesh from 2 squirrels into bite-sized pieces. Roll in seasoned flour and fry in 2oz (50g) fat or dripping with 4oz (100g) onions. Pour in brown stock, bring to the boil and stir carefully until a smooth, slightly thickened sauce results. Add 6oz (150g) carrots, 2-3 sticks of celery (cut), a sachet of bouquet garni and seasoning to taste. Cover with a well-fitting lid and simmer for $2\frac{1}{4}$-$2\frac{1}{2}$ hours. Serve in a hot dish or casserole.

The more discerning will note that I have given recipes where the squirrel has been cut up into small, almost unrecognisable fragments. This is necessary, especially when first trying out the dish on friends. Whole baked squirrel has the unfortunate tendency to look like a small cooked human, or worse still a rat, an appearance offensive to even the most courteous of guests.

One other point: squirrels are best avoided during the breeding season, when they have a definite 'bouquet' that few find appealing. *Bon appetit!*

Tree Barking

In most countries squirrels are shot and snared not for food, but because of the damage they cause, especially to growing trees. The creature has been blamed for a variety of other misdemeanours: stealing fruit, digging up bulbs, damaging houses and robbing birds' nests. In the

United Kingdom gamekeepers seem to regard nest-robbing and the killing of nestlings as the main reasons for trapping squirrels. There is no doubt some truth in all these accusations, especially nest-robbing. Shorten (1954) mentions such behaviour, and I have personally seen a grey squirrel stealthily approach a blackbird's nest three times (the nest contained two eggs), only to be driven off on each occasion by the parent bird. But all such unseemly behaviours are casual crimes; trees are the squirrel's main target.

Almost as soon as a tree is planted, squirrels both red and grey can be at work biting off the sweet, protein-rich lead shoots. The tree then no longer grows straight and true, but puts its growth into the lateral branches, producing what is known to foresters as a 'bushy top'. As such trees are almost worthless on the open market, the squirrel is at once placed high on the list of undesirables in any well-run plantation.

However this is not the worst crime attributed to the squirrel—the most heinous of all is barking which, as the name suggests, consists of removing the bark from trees, sometimes in considerable quantities. Trees are usually attacked between 10 and 50 years of age, and especially during the months of May and June (Tittensor, 1973). The bark itself is rarely eaten; the squirrel is after the salt-rich, nutritious vascular system (see page 60). Red squirrels seem to prefer barking conifers, while the grey confines its attention to broad-leaved deciduous trees. Barking damage from red squirrels has been reported from the British Isles (Shorten, 1954, 1957a), from Finland where it was calculated to be economically harmful to the country (Pullianen and Salonen, 1963), from many other parts of Scandinavia (Lundberg, 1946, Metzger, 1946) and also from central Europe (Altum, 1873, Turcek, 1959). The problem is not of recent origin; Harvie-Brown, wrote in 1880: 'Unanimously, my correspondents condemn the squirrel as one of the most destructive animals which frequent our forests.' In Britain red squirrels were hunted throughout the nineteenth and early twentieth centuries because of their destruction of young trees, primarily 10-50 year-old Scots pine.

There is little doubt that in Britain the grey squirrel too is responsible for a substantial amount of barking damage (Rowe, 1973). This normally occurs during the early summer (May and July) and generally

Red squirrel on tree (*Uno Berggren, Ardea Photographics*) ?

at time of high squirrel densities. There is also evidence that the barking of trees is used in its territorial display (Taylor, 1968). In addition, the grey squirrel has recently been implicated in the transmission of 'sooty bark' disease in sycamore trees. Spores from the fungus responsible for the infection were found in the animal's gut and also between the pads of both fore and hind feet (Abbott, Bevercombe and Rayner, 1977).

While the grey squirrel, in the United Kingdom, is by far the worst offender, this is simply because the red-squirrel population of these islands is so low that at present it makes no major impact on our forest resources. Pullianen (1963) and Pullianen and Salonen (1963) have described the red squirrel's method of bark stripping; in general the same account can be applied to the grey. The oldest trees, those 50-90 years old, were stripped in patches, while younger pines were stripped spirally, sometimes for considerable distances down the trunk. Shorten (1954) believes that both red and grey squirrels select the healthiest trees, which seems reasonable if they are to derive the greatest return from their efforts.

Occasionally, the trees may be ring-barked (stripped at the same height right round the trunk). This is fatal for growth, being sometimes used by foresters themselves to kill off a standing tree. In ring-barking the tree is deprived of the ability to transport its food products down the trunk, and water up to the leaves. Without water, photosynthesis in the leaves ceases and the tree above the barked area dies off. Squirrels usually ring-bark trees about three-quarters of the way up the trunk, so being sited towards the top of the tree, the damage is much less likely to be seen. The top quarter of the tree dies, and the first storm or strong wind snaps it from the rest of the trunk. Trees subjected to wind-snap are almost useless, especially where grown for height and straightness, for example conifer trees for telegraph poles or pit-props.

But even where barking does not completely circle the tree, the damage can be substantial. Tittensor (1974) reports a survey of red-squirrel damage on 63 wind-blown conifers in Edensmuir Forest, Scotland. The injury consisted of areas stripped of bark along the internodes of the crown of the tree. Though no tree had been com-

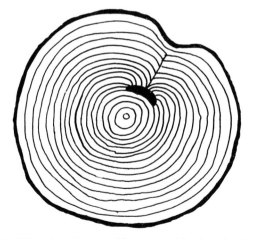

19. Pine wound caused by squirrel bark-stripping

121

pletely ring-barked, over a period of several years almost 80 per cent of the trees had been damaged, with an average of 7 stripping sites per tree. One tree had 28 zones stripped of bark! Given the size of the trees, the wounds inflicted by the squirrels were not particularly large, yet each was a serious blow to timber production. Unlike deciduous trees, the pines of Edensmuir (and other conifer species) are not able to heal squirrel damage. What happens is that as the tree grows it increases in diameter and the adjacent areas cover the wound, masking it from view. Although the tree now looks healthy, the covering layers never adhere to the surface of the wound and pockets of resin may form in the gap created. When cut down the tree appears perfect but at the sawmill the weakness will become obvious. As with a ring-barked tree, much of the timber will have to be scrapped.

So long as squirrel numbers are small and stable, damage to trees will be minimal, and forest managers are unlikely to take punitive action against the rodents. But in the British Isles grey-squirrel numbers are neither small nor stable. The animal is a pest, the most serious mammalian pest our forests have to face. Something has to be done to keep their population, and the damage they cause, to a minimum. If our woods and parklands were as thickly populated with squirrel predators as they are with *S.carolinensis*, the problem would most likely resolve itself: as squirrel numbers increased so would the predator population, thereby holding the prey species in check. But this is manifestly not the case. Although the grey in Britain does have enemies, these are mostly casual predators, far too uncommon to regulate successfully the squirrel population or to prevent their 'crimes' against the forest plantations. In the absence of any effective animal 'policeman', man himself must take a hand as a regulator of squirrel numbers.

10
Control and Culling

Both red and grey squirrel move from tree to tree via the connecting branches of the forest canopy. Even when the crowns of trees do not touch, the squirrel is still capable of bridging the gap by tremendous leaps. To prevent squirrel occupation of a tree, every branch on that tree must be at least 3m (9ft) from any other point of vantage. In forests and plantations economic factors make it impossible to allow such a large air-barrier; the trees are planted much closer together and their interlocking canopy is perfect for squirrel movement. It is therefore impossible to prevent squirrels colonising every suitable part of the wood.

Only with single trees or small stands of them is it possible to keep them away—by covering the trunk with a protective metal sleeve. This should be at least 1.5m (5ft) above ground level, and 0.75m (2½ft) in vertical height. Special care should be taken with the seam of the sleeve; squirrels are phenomenal climbers and if the seam is not perfectly smooth the animal will almost certainly use its irregularities to cross the metal barrier and take up residence in the 'protected' tree. A band of creosote painted around the trunk is also said to be an effective barrier.

Some organisations have taken even more unusual steps to keep the squirrel out of bounds. During the winter of 1978-9 hungry squirrels 'invaded' power stations belonging to the Massachusetts Power Company. The rodents foraged throughout the building, biting through insulation, or striking against electric cables with even worse effect. In the words of the American reporter who covered the story, 'Zap! No power, no squirrel.' The resulting blackouts paralysed large areas of Massachusetts causing inconvenience and potential danger to a multitude of users. It proved impossible to 'squirrel-proof' so large an installation and the company was completely nonplussed until one of its employees came up with an ingenious solution. The Masschusetts grey squirrel is terrified of owls, so the company bought a number of plastic (styrofoam) decoy owls and set them, like lonely sentinels, on prominent perches atop the buildings and on the surrounding fences. The response was virtually instantaneous. What had appeared an intractable problem vanished overnight; as soon as the 'owls' appeared no squirrel set foot inside the power station and the company's blackout rate decreased to more acceptable levels.

Protection of trees in this rather novel way is obviously possible for only a small proportion of any nation's forests (though it might be invaluable in small orchards or squirrel-ruined gardens), and it does nothing to control the size of the squirrel population. One way in which man does regulate the numbers of squirrels, and a host of other small mammals, is by his use of the motor car. No one can drive along country roads without seeing small corpses strewn across the road, lying sprawled in the gutter or collapsed on the roadside verge. Considering the high traffic-density in the British Isles nowadays, it is surprising that there has been little work done on vehicle-induced mortality, as has been done for some roads in the United States (Oxley, Fenton, and Carmody, 1974). These investigators found that over a period of 116 days 1 grey squirrel had been killed for every 4 miles of medium-width roadway. On the 78 miles of highway surveyed regularly, one squirrel was knocked down by a motor vehicle every 36 hours. As each region of road was monitored only once every eleven or twelve days, these road-casualty figures probably underestimate the mortality—scavenging mammals and birds would certainly have removed some of the corpses between surveys.

In addition, Oxley et al (1974) have shown that, although metalled roads may speed human traffic, once they have reached a certain width they act as a very effective barrier to the travels of small mammals and thus divide their population into 'islands' isolated from each other. Such a situation could easily fragment the gene pool of a number of small mammal species and, in the long term, weigh the scales against the survival of the species as a whole. This possibility has been totally

124

(*Above*) Grey squirrel with acorn (*Bridget Wheeler*); (*below*) Grey squirrels about to mate (*F. V. Blackburn*)

ignored by the planners of our ever-wider highways, especially the six-laned motorways. As an example of how roadways can isolate different sections of a mammal's population, Oxley and his co-workers suggest that a dual carriageway with a clearance of 90m (98yd) or more may be as effective a barrier as a body of water twice as wide!

But all these dangers are incidental, and if squirrel numbers are to be controlled within any given area of forest (to prevent damage to trees, etc), man must take a far more direct approach. Most authorities agree that we must put away all dreams of totally exterminating the grey squirrel in the United Kingdom. It is logistically impossible to organise squirrel destruction on a countrywide scale, even if it would be desirable and squirrels will infiltrate a controlled area from any region not subject to control. What can be done is to keep the population at a minimum, so that damage from squirrels remains at the lowest possible level. To do this man must actively seek out and destroy squirrels in large numbers during those times when they prove a positive danger to crops or trees. It is, for example, good policy to destroy grey squirrels between the months of May and July, when most barking damage occurs. Because of the high rate of emigration from surrounding areas into the population, it is a waste of time to cull the creature during any other month. Methods for controlling squirrel numbers fall into the unholy triad of trapping, poisoning and shooting.

Trapping

Trapping is probably the oldest method of catching squirrels or other small to medium-sized mammals. One of the most primitive ways is by snaring, in which the animal traps itself in a noose made of wire or cord. Over the centuries some extremely ingenious snares and trigger mechanisms have been devised to help the squirrel and related beasts on their way to oblivion (fig 20). Dead-fall traps (fig 21) in which the animal is crushed by some heavy weight, are equally primitive and just as effective. However, it takes many years of experience and a considerable amount of woodcraft to set these traps successfully on a

Pine seeds are the red's favourite food (*B. S. Turner*)

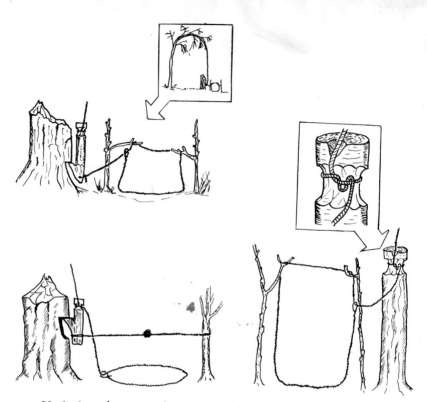

20. Activated snares and trigger mechanisms (after Petrides, 1946)

large scale; in today's world the emphasis is on speed and efficiency, not craft-skills. What is needed is a selection of humane traps—easy to position and set, and giving a high kill ratio even when used by an inexperienced trapper. Such devices are now readily available; they fall into two main types: live- and dead-traps.

Live-traps

There are a number of live-traps on the market; they are not everyone's choice, some people feeling that traps that kill the animal outright are more humane. The largest live trap is the Legg PB (Legg Permanently-Baited Multi-Capture Trap). With this device, it is possible to capture several squirrels at once, useful on those rare days when everything

21. Dead-fall traps (after Petrides, 1946)

goes right and squirrels seem to want nothing more than to get inside one's traps. It consists of three mesh tunnels or compartments lying side by side, the middle compartment holding the bait and opening into the tunnels on each side by means of a one-way door. Another one-way door lies at the entrance of the middle tunnel, through which the squirrels gain access to the trap. The tunnel sides and front of the trap are of solid metal so that the sight of those squirrels already captured will not deter others from entering. The animal enters, attracted by the whole-grain bait which lies below the floor of the middle compartment. Once inside, it finds itself unable to retreat the way it entered, or to avail itself of the bait which is protected by a mesh covering. It therefore moves forward through one of the two gates and so into either the left or right holding-tunnel.

Although quite an efficient trap, the Legg PB is bulky; it is difficult for a man to carry more than one trap at a time. The single-catch version, the Legg Midget, is essentially a Legg PB shorn of its two outer tunnels and the second one-way gate. It is therefore less than one-third the size of its bigger brother and far easier to manhandle. Its only disadvantage is that it only catches one squirrel, although on rare occasions a second unwary animal may enter after the first.

129

A similar trap is the Legg Single Trap; in this model the door is not one-way, but instead drops to close off the entrance whenever the squirrel displaces a wire treadle at the rear of the cage. The Fuller Bullseye Trap, a small cylindrical plastic device, works on the same drop-door principle.

Whether the one-way trap is more efficient than the drop-door model is hotly disputed among those who study or trap squirrels. Some insist the one-way door is far more reliable, citing instances when a squirrel has entered a drop-door cage, tripped the release treadle, and then made off scot-free after eating the bait, the door of the trap having failed to fall because twigs or dirt had blocked the runnels. Others counter that this undoubted disadvantage is offset by the greater number of squirrels who enter a drop-door trap, where there is no obstacle to them reaching their goal—the bait. By contrast squirrels approaching a one-way door have to push against the metal of the door in order to enter, something not all animals are keen to do.

On balance, probably both types of trap are equally efficient over a given period; indeed it is sometimes preferable to use both types together as this tends to increase the 'bag'. But whatever their merits and demerits, both suffer from the same disadvantages: they must always be sited on level ground so that the doors function efficiently, and they must be pegged or weighted down securely.

Anyone who has seen a squirrel in a trap will know just how active and powerful his attempts to escape can be. In addition, the material of which traps are usually manufactured is by no means impregnable to squirrel attack. When trapping in Thetford Chase, I remember being informed by one experienced trapper that the cage we were approaching definitely contained a captive. And indeed it had, but the squirrel in question had managed to gnaw a good-sized hole through the thick metal mesh and made good its escape!

Trapping Craft

Although these live-catching devices are much easier to handle than snares or dead-fall traps, a fair amount of expertise is required if the kill is to be substantial. The site for the trap should be carefully chosen: the best location is at the base of a tree known to be used by squirrels travelling regularly between the canopy and the ground. The site itself should preferably be clear of growth and, if possible, the trap should be positioned on a carpet of fallen leaves. Camouflage the trap whenever practicable; it gives some protection to the captive animal and helps to hide the trap from human eyes and so discourages vandalism.

How many traps are used depends on a variety of factors including the type of crop to be protected, its size and shape, the number of squirrels attacking it and the sort of woodland from which they make their sallies. As in any war, it always pays to know as much as you can about the enemy, and any extra intelligence, such as knowledge of a drainage ditch down which many animals pass during the day, is sure to pay dividends in terms of extra squirrels caught. In general, multi-catch traps should be sited 150-200m (164-219yd) apart, single-catch traps about one-third to one-half this distance. Twenty traps make up a convenient trap-line, and in one day four such lines can be visited provided each line is set fairly close to the next.

It is as well not to set the trap to 'catch' immediately; better results

Trapping and collaring ⚲

are obtained if the squirrels are allowed to get used to the trap and to collecting food from it. This is done by pre-baiting the trap with whatever bait is to be used. Yellow whole maize is the usual bait, but any whole-grain cereal will serve. The bait should be strewn copiously around the trap and its environs up to a distance of about 2m (2·2yd). A double-handful is placed inside the trap and at the entrance. After two days the bait should be examined to see if the squirrels have been visiting the site: if the whole grain has been removed or if most of the husk has been eaten, the culprits are probably birds and mice respectively. Only if the germ of the maize has been consumed and the floury husk left relatively intact, has the bait been attacked by squirrels.

Once it is certain that squirrels are visiting the trap a second helping of maize is offered, this time only at the entrance and inside the trap. After a further two days only the bait inside the trap is replenished, and in addition the trap is set for its first victim. Each trap should now be visited at least once a day to prevent suffering to the trapped animal, and once a squirrel is found captured, it must be despatched as rapidly as possible. This is very difficult to achieve while the squirrel is in the trap, and it is usually transferred to a bag or sack by holding the open end of the sack over the door of the trap and allowing the animal to run into it. When safely transferred it is an easy matter to coax the beast, head first, into a corner of the sack when it can be painlessly and efficiently killed by a sharp blow on the head with a bludgeon.

Dead-traps
A more humane method of disposing of squirrels is to use a dead-trap. These work on the same principle as the familiar mouse-trap, killing the creature instantly, usually by some double-bladed jaw which crushes the squirrel across the head or body. Traps such as the Juby, Imbra, Bawyer and Lloyd models are of this type and are commonly used in the United Kingdom. In 1957, the Conibear trap was introduced (Collier, 1957) for the taking of squirrel- to beaver-sized animals. This model is extremely effective as it can be set in various positions.

The British-made models must be sited on level ground and (in accordance with the Pests Act 1954, and the Protection of Birds Act 1954) in tunnels, so that no birds and few other mammal species are placed at risk. The tunnels may be natural hollows in tree trunks, drainage pipes or walls. Alternatively, special artificial tunnels can be constructed with bricks, pipes, turf or any other solid material that comes to hand. The tunnel should be around 600mm (24in) long and just broad and high enough to allow the arms of the trap to strike without hindrance. One excellent means of tunnel construction is to drive stakes into the ground at an angle with a large tree trunk, and close the entrance further with small branches. Wherever possible the trap should be sited with the treadle level with the tunnel floor.

Bait is not essential with dead-traps, the animal's natural curiosity leading it to explore the tunnel. However a small amount placed near the entrance will bring the squirrel closer to the trap sooner.

Poisoning

Trapping squirrels may seem cruel, but at least the animal dies quickly and painlessly, which is more than can be said for the second method of control—poisoning. The most commonly used chemicals in the fight against the squirrel are the anti-coagulants. As their name suggests, they prevent coagulation of the blood, meaning that the blood of any animal which ingests sufficient quantities of the poison will be unable to clot. They become, in effect, haemophiliacs. As with sufferers from the natural form of the disease, in chemically-induced haemophilia any internal haemorrhage, no matter how small, will lead to death from massive and unstoppable internal bleeding. Because the incidence of minor internal haemorrhages is high in most mammals, including both the squirrel and ourselves, a substantial reduction can be made in squirrel numbers if one can persuade enough squirrels to feed from the poisoned bait.

Warfarin, well-known as a rat poison, is the most frequently used anti-coagulant against squirrels, though others such as coumachlor, fumarin and valone are also favoured in some countries (Bentley, 1966). There are, however, several complications. The squirrels must take the poison on several consecutive days before they will succumb. There is also the risk that other wildlife, such as the endemic red squirrel, may inadvertently consume lethal quantities. The Grey

Squirrels (Warfarin) Order 1973 made under the Agriculture (Miscellaneous Provisions) Act 1972 defines the use of warfarin in grey-squirrel control.

The species most at risk (apart from the grey) is the red squirrel. Other mammals, such as the bank-vole, (*Clethrionomys glareolus*), may also die from the poison, but not in sufficient numbers to affect the stability of their populations as a whole. Neither does poisoning appear to affect numbers of predators such as owls, foxes or stoats. The excluded counties list was compiled primarily to safeguard those areas where red squirrels still survive without grey competition; in regions of grey/red interface it is recommended that warfarin should not be used, lest red as well as grey succumb.

As the red squirrel is smaller than the grey it is very difficult to devise an efficient method of presenting poisoned wheat to the introduced species without it also attracting our native squirrel. To minimise the risks to it and other wildlife, legislation firmly regulates hopper construction: although the hopper carrying the poison bait can be of any reasonable size, access to the bait must be through a long (approximately 250mm [10in]) tunnel. This greatly decreases the number of species that might take the bait simply because it is there. An efficient design of poison hopper is shown in fig 22.

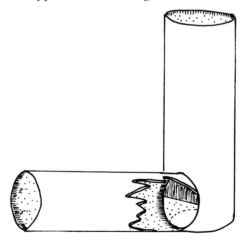

22. Recommended design of poison hopper

134

Hopper location is governed by the same criteria as the siting of single-catch, live-trap cages, with similar precautions with regard to pegging the structure securely to the ground. One important additional precaution, especially when the hoppers are used on land frequented by the general public, is clearly to label each site with a large and clearly legible POISON notice.

As with the tunnel-sited dead-traps, a handful of whole maize grains spread round the hopper entrance will attract squirrels from a distance and ensure they take the poisoned bait more quickly.

Poisoning is not perhaps as efficient as live or dead trapping, nor does it give the same satisfaction to those engaged in the work; its great advantage lies in the small number of men required to work the system and therefore its low cost. Poisoning, using a 2.5kg (5½lb) reservoir of bait involves only one weekly visit, whereas trap-lines must be attended at least once a day.

Shooting

Shooting is probably the least effective, though to many people the most enjoyable, method of killing squirrels. Its obvious inadequacy can be judged from the success or otherwise of the 'squirrel clubs', formed for no other purpose than to bring about the destruction of as many members of the Sciuridae as they possibly could. In Scotland and the border countries a bounty system was tried out during the late 1800s. On the Cawdor estates the price on each red squirrel's head, or rather, tail, was 3d or 4d. Spurred by this financial reward, up to 1,200 squirrels were killed in a single season, and over a period of seventeen years 14,123 tails were presented for payment. Although the numbers killed seemed high, the total red-squirrel population suffered no great permanent decline.

This sobering fact does not seem to have discouraged others. In the early 1900s, a number of large Scottish estates joined together to form the Highland Squirrel Club; this organisation accounted for more than 82,000 red squirrels between 1903 and 1933, with no noticeable effect on the general red-squirrel population. At about the same time as the Highland Squirrel Club was giving up the fight against S. vulgaris, other groups were being organised in many British counties with the grey squirrel as their target. Many thousands of greys were shot by members with free cartridges provided by the County Agricultural Executive Committees. Despite this, grey squirrels continue to thrive throughout the country.

Some people still shoot squirrels simply by stalking them. Several different types of gun can 'take out' the grey squirrel, including the .410 shotgun (at close range) and the .22 cartridge rifle (especially with the modern expanding 'varmint' bullets); but by far the best squirrel-killer is the 12-bore shotgun. A single-barrel model will do, but squirrels are tricky targets and it is probably better to use side-by-side or automatic guns when hunting them.

Getting a clear shot at such elusive targets is always a problem; one ruse that works especially well was told me by Bridget Wheeler, a wildlife photographer living in Kent. As soon as it feels itself threatened, a squirrel will move around to the far side of a tree-trunk, so that the solid security of a foot or so of timber stands between it and its potential enemy. Periodically it peeks round the trunk, moving if the potential threat changes its position so that there is always that nice thick tree between squirrel and menace. The shooter can use this behaviour to his own advantage by carrying a forked branch some 1.5-1.8m (5-6ft) long. When he knows he has been spotted by the squirrel, the hunter drives the stick firmly into the ground, places his hat and jacket on the upright branch and then moves off to the opposite side from which the squirrel is making its periodic observations. The squirrel peers round the tree, sees what it thinks is its enemy in exactly the same position as before, and likewise stays put behind the protective bulwark of the trunk. The hunter can then move stealthily around the tree until he has the chance of a clear shot.

A less 'sporting' method of controlling the grey squirrel by shooting is drey-poking. Essentially, the idea is to attack the squirrel while it is at home in its drey and to shoot it as it attempts to flee. To do this, long light-weight (usually tubular-aluminium) poles are used. The poles normally comprise ten 2m (6½ft) sections which can be joined together by spring clips. A hook-top for dislodging the drey completes the equipment. Drey-poking is a group exercise, needing at least five men

Alert squirrel

to make it effective. One, or preferably two, men use the poles against the dreys while the remainder get ready to pot the unfortunate squirrel as soon as it tries to escape. It is also very useful to possess a good gun-dog who can take any wounded squirrel that falls to the ground and would otherwise escape. In North America, many dogs are trained to follow a squirrel trail and 'point' the tree in which a squirrel is hiding. Wounded squirrels seeking cover on the ground can also be located with the help of a dog.

Such a large workforce inevitably makes drey-poking expensive, unless one can drum up support for a shoot from among the local hunting fraternity. This is often difficult, especially as drey-poking is most effective during wet, cold windy weather when, like the squirrel, most humans are happiest tucked up safely in their own homes. As with other forms of hunting, experience is an invaluable aid to success. It is best if the men handling the poles do not strike the drey too hard; violent blows often result in all the squirrels in the drey making a run for it at the same time. The chances of hitting three or four squirrels with one or two guns is not very high, and it is better if the drey is struck gently, almost tenderly, at first. The squirrels will then be more curious than alarmed and often leave the drey singly and much more slowly than if the drey has been subject to a vigorous assault from the drey-poker.

Each drey in the forest should be investigated, even those which appear unused, for squirrels, hearing the sound of possible danger as the men enter the woods, will often seek the nearest drey regardless of its condition, as a handy hideout. If the animal does manage to leave the vicinity of the nest, it will almost invariably avoid the drey-pole and take to the opposite side of the tree. If a gun is stationed opposite the drey-poker (with the tree between them), such squirrels are easy to pick off.

Drey-poking suffers from even more disadvantages than the other methods of grey-squirrel control. It can only be successfully carried out when the trees are without leaves, that is between early winter and springtime. Any reduction in the squirrel population during this time will have only a brief effect in depressing squirrel numbers because of their high rate of movement around this time. Research has shown that the main season for tree-barking is between May and July, a time when the trees are coming into full bloom and the squirrel dreys are very hard to see. Even if it were possible to drey-poke during spring and early summer, the high rate of dispersal and squirrel movement during this period would effectively recolonise an area that has been shot out within four to eight weeks.

Drey-poking may be at the less efficient end of the control spectrum, but it has to be admitted that no system or combination of systems has at present any chance of removing the grey squirrel from the British countryside, or even affecting its numbers to the extent that the beast might become rare. Nevertheless, there are other possibilities.

Biological Control

One method that has not been tried on squirrels in this country is biological control, where the pest species' numbers are controlled by the use of a second species. In essence, biological control tries to mimic the balance of nature found in the wild, where each prey species lives in equilibrium with its predators, with neither increasing to unmanageable proportions. Biological control is usually brought in where man has destroyed a pest's natural predators, introduced the pest into areas where no natural predators exist, or manipulated the environment to such a degree that the population of a pest species becomes unregulated and therefore climbs to unnaturally high numbers which then threaten the environment.

Many parts of the world now show examples of such control, though perhaps none so completely as the Caribbean island of Barbados. When first discovered it was named Los Barbados 'The Bearded' for the great number of bearded figs that once covered most of the island. The first English colonists arrived in 1627, and within a few decades the fig, and the rest of the forest trees were gone, and in their place stood extensive forests of sugar cane, planted and managed by man. To the sugar-cane borer, a weevil whose larva delights in feeding off the stems of sugar cane, these forests comprised an almost infinite supply of food. The weevil population rocketed to plague proportions, so that almost the entire cane crop was in danger of disappearing into the maws of the weevil's insatiable larvae. Fortunately, in the 1940s scientists investigating the possiblity of biological control discovered a braconid wasp which parasitises the larva of the sugar-cane borer by injecting its own egg into the larva's body; the wasp egg hatches and the resulting larva literally eats the sugar-cane borer alive. As each adult wasp produces scores of eggs, the weevil's larvae are killed off in huge numbers. When this wasp (bred artificially) was released into Bajan fields the menace was quickly contained and within a few years damage from the weevil was minimal.

How does this relate to squirrels? There is, unfortunately, no wasp or other insect vector who can perform such an efficient job of destruction on our unwanted sciurids but, as we have seen in Chapter 8, there are predators who can perform much the same function. Casual predators such as the stoat or fox will not greatly decrease grey-squirrel numbers, but both the wild cat and the pine marten could very well do just that. Sadly the wild cat has had a very bad press with the general public who feel (wrongly) that it is a nasty, savage and altogether unpredictable beast. Public opinion would probably prevent its reintroduction over wide areas of the United Kingdom. The pine marten is a very different matter; this lithe attractive creature has not been branded as 'vicious'. It is primarily an arboreal predator and would seek most of its food in the tree-tops, unlike the wild cat who would undoubtedly take chickens, homing pigeons and pedigree Yorkshire terriers if given half a chance. Moreover the pine marten is a true native of the British Isles and formerly widely distributed throughout the country, so there is no sound ecological argument against its reintroduction.

Because the grey squirrel is very common in many parts of the British Isles, the pine marten would certainly turn its attention to this species first. Its daily intake of food is about 10 per cent of its body weight, ie about 120g (4oz) of meat per day on average (Schmidt, 1943). If, as Hoglund (1960) discovered, the pine marten's diet is composed of 51 per cent squirrel, then approximately 60g (2oz) of squirrel is eaten each day. Grey squirrel weigh on average 550g (19oz) so one pine marten will kill one squirrel every 9 days, ie about 40 squirrels each year, a figure far in excess of even the most efficient trap.

If the grey squirrel population declined under the pressure of marten predation, the mustelid might then change its tactics and include more, for example, voles, in its diet. This is really beside the point, but it has been given as a reason for not introducing the pine marten. If the marten changed its diet it would be because the squirrel population had declined to such a low level that alone it could no longer support the marten population; this surely is what we want—a low population of grey squirrels. And we can be sure that if their numbers increased again, the martens would be there to mop up the surplus.

It is now accepted that the grey squirrel will not be exterminated in Britain by any control measure yet available, so surely it makes sense to hold down their numbers without recourse to labour-intensive methods which have been shown to be ineffective and which also pose a threat to other British wildlife. There is no valid reason why the pine marten should not be reintroduced.

Birth Control

Another method of biological control which has been effective with insects, but which has never to my knowledge been used with small mammals, is birth control. In several species of insect pests, one sex or the other has been rendered infertile, so that when the sterile individual mates with a fertile member of the opposite sex, the putative offspring fail to develop and the next generation is reduced commensurately.

Given our knowledge of the hormonal factors involved in mammalian reproduction (especially in rodents such as the white laboratory-rat), it should not be beyond the wit of man to devise some sort of 'birth pill' which could be fed to the female grey squirrel. It should also be possible to use the existing poison hoppers to feed squirrels a contraceptive chemical spread evenly over wheat grain, in the same way that grain poisoned by warfarin is prepared. There is even a chance that the contraceptive could be made species, or at least genus, specific, so that it would affect squirrels alone and perhaps only the grey squirrel.

If such a method was used on a wide enough scale, the older, more established control methods (used in conjunction with the birth-control technique) would become more effective. The contraceptive pill would reduce the numbers of the next generation of grey squirrels, thereby colonisation from surrounding areas (the main bugbear of any control programme) would be likewise reduced and the 'clout' of trapping, poisoning or even shooting would be greatly increased. It might yet be possible to hold the tide against the grey menace and to give our own species, the native red squirrel, a chance to regroup and perhaps even make a come-back.

Until that time, we had better learn to live with the grey squirrel. We *could* make a virtue out of necessity by ceasing to regard it as simply a pest and instead consider it a valuable game animal. In the United States, as already mentioned, this is certainly the case; during 1962, in the state of Ohio, almost 1½ *million* squirrels were shot for sport (Donohoe, 1965). Perhaps if we were to ask for British squirrel-hunters

141

we would find many ready to oblige. The sale of air-rifles in the United Kingdom now runs at an annual 5,000 guns each year, many of them .22 calibre and ideal for squirrel shooting.

Instead of many of these young men spending their time blowing the heads and wings off sparrows and blackbirds, they could be helping to keep an acknowledged forest pest in check, preserving trees from damage and, by reducing the need for imported timber, saving Britain valuable foreign exchange. Many would even pay for the privilege!

Squirrel drey (*F. V. Blackburn*)

11
How Squirrels are Studied

Throughout this book we have used the information brought us by the many naturalists and scientists whose diligence, perseverance and sheer hard work have contributed to a further understanding of the squirrel's behaviour and biology. From the time of the early enthusiasts for natural history, like Gilbert White, a portrait of the squirrel's life has gradually been painted, each student adding a few more brush strokes to the canvas until we have seen that what was simply a pretty part of our fauna is really a living, breathing creature, developing, growing, feeding and interacting both with other members of its species and with its environment. So far, we have interested ourselves only with the results of their studies, and not with the methods by which the secrets of the squirrel were uncovered.

Imagine oneself faced with a totally new species of mammal: to understand the creature even partially one must discover a multitude of facts about it and about its existence within the niche it inhabits. The beast must be described, its range, population size and density elucidated, as well as the secrets of its feeding, reproduction and predation, its development from infancy, its social behaviour and much more. Fortunately, there are a battery of techniques which make this formidable task less daunting.

One of the first things is to capture a member of the species, preferably when it is very young, and to hand-rear it. If this is accomplished, a huge amount of information on development will be obtained. This was the method used by Horwich to study the development of motor behaviour in the grey squirrel. Body weight and increases in the size of

Grey squirrel cleaning after mating (*F. V. Blackburn*)

various parts of the body can also be measured. Tittensor (1970) did this for body weight and then used the information to make tentative estimates of the age of wild-caught squirrels trapped during his PhD study.

It is also possible to study the way in which the environment affects development. We have already seen how deprivation experiments can show some aspects of the squirrel's behaviour to be 'programmed' and almost totally independent of experience or prior learning (page 63). But other experiments have helped to redress the balance. Iraneus Eibl-Eibesfeldt (1967) studied the way in which the red squirrel develops its expertise in opening hard-shelled nuts such as hazel. Adult squirrels open hazel nuts by gnawing a neat furrow from the base to the top of the nut, or *vice versa*, following a shallow groove on the nut's more flattened side. By contrast, young squirrels seem completely 'at sea' when faced with a similar problem. They gnaw furrows at a furious rate all over the rind until the shell eventually breaks. As they grow older, this waste of effort is reduced until the adult opening pattern is reached. But the question remains: is this more efficient technique due to a maturation of the nervous system which, when old enough, possesses an 'inbuilt answer', or does the squirrel learn the solution to this problem from its own experience of opening nuts?

To answer this, Eibl-Eibesfeldt raised 23 squirrels under conditions which denied them both the opportunity to watch other squirrels opening nuts and the chance to open nuts themselves. At the age of 4 to 6 months, each squirrel was given its first nut and the reactions noted. All the animals were interested but showed a clear lack of skill in opening the nut and even in handling it. They all gnawed at the object in their hands and almost all learned the technique after they had opened between 7 and 20. At first each nut took 15 or 20 minutes to crack, but once the squirrels had discovered the splitting technique, 2 to 3 minutes was the norm. This experiment shows that squirrels have to learn the technique for opening nuts (otherwise the first nut would have been opened as quickly as the twentieth). They are equipped with the movements for gnawing and splitting but, by trial and error, they must *learn* how best to place the furrow.

So, in this case the squirrel is not simply a biological computer, fulfilling a preordained programme when placed in a suitable situation. It can learn from experience in much the same way as a human learns to chop firewood by striking with the axe-blade parallel to the grain of the wood and not across it. But *Homo sapiens* can also discover the best means to chop wood simply by watching another man do it. Recent experiments have shown that such observational learning is also not above some members of the Sciuridae.

E. V. Hanson and P. D. Weigl of Wake Forest University demonstrated this in the American red squirrel, *Tamiasciurus hudsonicus*, by a simple, elegant experiment which would have been impossible to arrange had their subjects not been captive animals. They took a number of squirrels who had never experienced feeding with nuts, and divided them into two groups visually isolated from one another. One group (group A) was given nuts for the first time and their responses observed. The other squirrels (group B) were likewise given hickory nuts but, in addition, were allowed to watch an experienced squirrel

Squirrel eating

(the model) feeding on the same nuts. After six weeks, it was found that group B expended only half the energy of group A when opening the nuts, while their time and technique approached the model far more closely than the no-model group A. The improved performance persisted after the model had been removed. These workers believe that young squirrels learn many of their behaviours more efficiently by taking their parents as a model.

To understand the food requirements of the squirrel one has to know just how efficiently it extracts energy from what it eats. This can be done by using a bomb calorimeter to measure the potential amount of energy in, say, 5g of nuts. A captive squirrel is then fed a similar quantity and its droppings collected; by placing the faeces in a bomb calorimeter the amount of energy remaining (and therefrore *not* extracted by the squirrel) can be determined. Using this or similar information, it is possible to calculate just how much food a squirrel needs to remain active and healthy over a range of different environmental conditions, and to calculate how much natural food it will need to consume at different seasons of the year in order to stay alive (Short and Duke, 1971).

Squirrel Population Study

Although such experiments are useful, there is always a slight suspicion that, albeit inadvertently, the experimenter has done something to bias the results one way or the other. Simply by hand-rearing the squirrel, a number of subtle stimuli may be lacking—the experimenter cannot, after all, lick the infant squirrel or handle it in exactly the same way as a mother squirrel. Where such natural factors are lacking or unobtainable, we must make do with this slightly suspect information, but where there is any chance that data can be collected in the wild as opposed to in a laboratory, then every scientist should don his anorak and wellingtons and follow the squirrel into its natural habitat. Indeed, many aspects of the squirrel's biology can only be understood by means of field observations.

Once in the field, one of the first measurements to make is the size of the squirrel population within a specified area. Only by knowing this important fact is it possible to decide if, for example, the number of squirrels constitutes a threat to the hardwood plantation in which they are living, or possibly to a nearby field of corn. Population estimation is fraught with pitfalls, but one of the most successful and widely used methods is the Peterson or Lincoln Index. The method involves catching a segment of the animal species concerned, individually marking the creatures, and then estimating the total population size from the frequency of recapture of these marked animals.

If n = total number of individuals captured, and t = the total number of captures (t and n will be different as some animals will be caught more than once) then it is possible to estimate the total population (N) by using the following formula:

$$N = \frac{n}{1-(n/t)}$$

The Lincoln Index can be invalidated by several factors. Taylor (1975) has shown that different traps will catch different types of grey squirrel (either residents or migrants), producing a trap bias which would tend to make the estimate inaccurate. Weather conditions may also produce the same effect. However if such factors are allowed for, the Lincoln Index can give a fairly accurate assessment of population size, allowing the researcher to follow the dynamics of population increase and decrease over the years and perhaps to relate such fluctuations to the presence or absence of predators, or to a scarcity or peak in the food supply.

Other aspects of general population information can be obtained by shooting or dead-trapping squirrels and examining their stomach contents. Though difficult to analyse, such information helps us to understand what the squirrel eats in the wild as opposed to its diet in captivity. The two are rarely the same—an infant orang-utan I home-reared for over fourteen months ate pork stew, drank tea and went wild over milk-chocolate buttons: hardly a reliable indication of the diet of its wild relatives! Squirrels captured for stomach-content analysis can also be examined for the parasites they harbour, while postmortems can give valuable indications of the diseases to which the Sciuridae are prone. Even the teeth of dead animals need not be wasted; Naumov (1934) has described a method by which differences in wear on the squirrel's cheek teeth can be used to estimate the age of any wild squirrel.

Studying Individual Animals

By virtue of their experimental design, studies on the general population can only give us general information. Those students interested in *detail*, who concern themselves with what happens to the squirrel as an individual, must use different methods of investigation. The most basic of these is simple observation (married to a good deal of experienced woodcraft). Using this technique, Tittensor (1974) discovered that not all the pine cones which the red squirrel eats are treated in the same way. Some cones are sniffed at and rejected, perhaps because of infestation by the boring insect larvae of *Dioryctria*, one of the few invertebrates against which the red squirrel has to compete for its supply of pine seed. The *size* of the cone is also important, those smaller than 30mm (1in) or larger than 50mm (2in) were not as readily taken as those occupying the 30-50mm (1-2in) range. Probably longer cones are chosen because of the greater seed quantity per cone, but increased size and weight create difficulties in manipulation, especially for a squirrel balanced precariously in the tree canopy. Intermediate-sized cones are therefore selected, the squirrels combining the advantages of feeding from larger cones with the greater safety involved in handling smaller ones.

If one wishes to go even deeper into the private life of the squirrel family, to pry for example on the secrets of their social behaviour, then the principal problem one faces is in distinguishing which animal is which. With some creatures this is fairly easy. Jane Goodall (1969) had no difficulty in telling one chimpanzee from the next, probably because of the striking resemblance of the chimp's face to our own physiognomy. But other animals can also be distinguished. Ian Douglas-Hamilton (1972) used the tears and frayed edges of elephant ears as a method of identification during his study of the African elephant.

Collaring ?

But with squirrels, the behavioural scientist is up against a far more difficult problem. It is possible to tell adult squirrels from juvenile members of the species and, in some seasons, to differentiate male from female, but I know of no person skilled enough to distinguish a group of squirrels individually. This is not surprising; to human eyes at least, one squirrel is very much the same as any other. They are also small, fast, and above all arboreal in their habits. Even if, at a distance of 4·5 or 9 metres (5 or 10yd) one could train oneself to observe the tiny facial and bodily differences that distinguish Joe squirrel from Fred squirrel, it would be a very different story when one tried to observe the same beasts engaging in a hostile encounter 10m (35ft) up in the forest canopy. What is needed is some method of making the squirrels look less alike so that individual animals can be identified instantly during the brief encounters that characterise most fieldwork. Such a requirement naturally involves marking the animals to be observed, and for this trapping once again comes into its own.

The animals are caught by means of live-trap cages, and transferred to some sort of holding device (usually a wire cone or a mesh bag) for marking. One basic requirement is to divide the squirrels into male and female animals, usually by clipping the tail. This appendage is a very distinctive part of a squirrel's anatomy and is therefore ideal for identification purposes. The distal half of the female's tail is shorn of all hair, while the male loses the hair at the base-half of the tail. In most cases this sexing is useful but it does not give enough detailed information for some researchers. They need *individual* markings, and these are obtained by a variety of inventive techniques, all of which depend either on the colour or location of marking to create a series of 'coded' combinations. Thompson (1977) used individually colour- and shape-coded plastic tags permanently attached to the ears of his squirrels. With this help he was able to analyse many facets of the grey squirrel's social system (Thompson 1977*a*, *b*, *c*). Jonathan Reynolds of the University of East Anglia, whose research was described in Chapter 4, colour-codes his squirrels by means of plastic collars on to which coloured 'beads' are strung in different combinations. In both these studies the animals must still be observed at fairly close range, as the distinctive markings added by the researchers are small and difficult to see from a distance.

R. H. Horwich (1972) overcame these problems by making the whole squirrel his marker. This worker divided the squirrel's body into a chequerboard of seven separately numbered sections (fig 23). Once caught, each squirrel was painted, according to this numbered system, with a preparation of Nyanzol A purple dye (Fitzwater, 1944). Up to three of the pelage sections were painted (eg the first squirrel caught might have area 1 painted, the sixteenth caught areas 2, 3, and 4, and so on). Scores of combinations are possible with this system and, so long as the beast is visible, it is usually possible to identify it correctly.

But even this inventive system has limitations if the researcher is interested in what an individual squirrel does on an hour-to-hour or even minute-to-minute basis. Colour-coded squirrels are recognisable when one can see them, but the problem is that they have the annoying

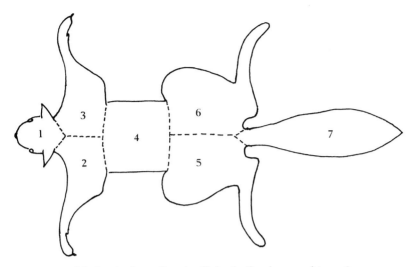

23. Sectioning of squirrel's body for dye-marking ?

habit of disappearing among the leaves and branches of the canopy almost as soon as they are spotted. And it may be hours, days or even weeks before that particular squirrel is seen again. If it leaves the area altogether, days can be wasted in fruitless searching.

For many years this was an unsolved problem. Then around 1962 came the first reports that it was possible to locate animals at a distance using sophisticated electronic equipment, a technique termed radio-location telemetry (Brander and Cochran, 1971). What happens is that the animal under study is fitted with a transmitter package (consisting of a power cell and a transmitter) slung from the animal's body by some form of harness. The transmitter broadcasts a radio signal which can be picked up by any observer tuned in to the wavelength of the transmitting radio 'beacon'. If the objective is to locate the animal in order to observe it, the observer simply homes on this beacon with a receiver and directional antenna until experience indicates that a spotting scope should be used to pick out the creature.

If the researcher does not wish to risk scaring off his subject, he can locate the animal by triangulation, obtaining his 'fix' by taking bearings on the signal from two or more locations. So useful is radio-telemetry in the study of animal behaviour that knowledge of the system is almost *de rigueur* for any self-respecting behavioural scientist.

In the squirrel this technique has proved its worth in several situations: it was only by using radio-telemetry that Nixon, Beal and Donohoe were able to discover the exact location of the female squirrel's breeding nest, and then to monitor her transfer of the young to a second drier nest (Chapter 7).

Though many of the squirrel's secrets can be uncovered only by the application of sophisticated statistical analysis or the use of electronic 'hardware', there is still much to be learnt from simpler, more traditional methods of observation. In squirrel biology it is still possible for the interested layman to discover important new facts about its life style. This is especially true now that the grey squirrel has become such a permanent part of suburban life.

12
Friends and Neighbours

The grey squirrel is well known in many towns throughout central and southern England. The creatures need very few trees to feel at home, and if they can charm their food from animal-starved suburbanites they can exist in fair numbers in areas that would otherwise be classified as extremely marginal habitats. House sparrows do much the same.

The grey squirrel is able to overcome its natural aversion to man and, to its own advantage, will adopt many unusual behaviours. While researching this book, I came across a number of these adaptable house squirrels, some of which were on to a very cushy number indeed. Amanda Collins, a secretary with the TV wildlife programme, 'Survival', told me about Nutkin, a female squirrel who visits her house regularly. The first Amanda knows is when the squirrel appears on its favourite perch, an ornamental concrete pillar. It then scrambles along the kitchen wall and, if the door is opened, enters boldly and waits fearlessly for its usual rations—a nice big biscuit. Coconut macaroons are preferred, but Nutkin is not averse to digestives or even a humble water biscuit! Nutkin eats her biscuit in a ritual manner, slowly turning it in her hands as she gnaws so that the circular shape is maintained down to the very last crumb. On several occasions an open door to the living room has given the family the pleasure of Nutkin's company for much longer than they expected. Trying to dislodge a well-satisfied squirrel from its warm perch at the top of one's curtains is far more difficult than most people imagine.

Nutkin becomes pregnant at least once a year, and as soon as the babies are weaned, loses no time in initiating them into the pleasures of suburban living. The youngsters at first remain on the ornamental

A suburban food-beggar ?

pillar watching mother's visit to this rodent equivalent of a soup-kitchen, but they very soon lose their initial anxiety and quickly learn to feed from the hand—thereby getting the most from their human neighbours. Presumably they then go off and try the same trick wherever they happen to set up home. One thing is certain, having tasted the *dolce vita*, it is unlikely they will move far from a built-up area.

Even the timid red can overcome its fear of humans, given sufficient time. M. H. Crawford tells a delightful tale of an invalid woman whose life was enlivened by house-calls from these beautiful creatures:

> She had a sitting room on the ground floor, and, with the door wide open, spent hours in making their acquaintance. She placed a bird table on the lawn, with food she knew they liked. The table was brought gradually day by day, nearer and nearer to her window. The Squirrels

came and helped themselves, gaining confidence at every visit. Finally, the table was placed right inside the room. Still they came. At last they were so friendly that if they found the window closed in the morning they would tap on it till it was opened.

But the story of the suburban squirrel is not unalloyed joy; for many householders the squirrel is a pain in the neck, or rather in the pocket. If the creature decides that a house roof is an eminently better site for a drey than some cold draughty tree-branch, conflict between human and rodent is inevitable. The results of a squirrel setting up home in your house can range from minor annoyance to major damage and costly repairs. The list of damage is long: lawns may be dug up, fruit patches raided, and attacks on everything that sticks up, hangs down or grows may become commonplace. In the USA and to a lesser degree in Britain, the grey squirrel causes quite severe structural damage. Lead cables are favoured sharpening stones for the squirrel's incisors, while co-axial leads from TV aerials can be ripped to shreds. The 'cute creature' makes a sudden transformation from semi-pet to total pest, and the rodent operator is often called in to try to combat the menace.

If squirrels have already taken up residence in the attic, it is essential to remove them before attempting to 'proof' the house against their return. Poisoning is not recommended. In most homes the squirrel will live in places very difficult for humans to reach, and the poisoned animal is very likely to die in an inaccessible part of the house, giving rise to a king-sized odour problem! Paradichlorobenzene crystals and naphthalene flakes which give off an 'anti-squirrel smell', are particularly recommended for squirrel eviction, especially in small enclosed spaces such as lofts.

John C. Jones, an American expert in this field, gives some additional advice: if young are present in the loft, a squirrel will not hesitate to attack when attempts are made to evict it, 'and squirrels can bite. Be prepared to defend against such an attack'. Once the squirrels have been sent packing, all entry holes under the eaves in louvres, ventilation spaces and suchlike must be closed. Do not neglect the chimney: squirrels have entered a house through the chimney and wreaked havoc on furniture and woodwork while the lawful occupants were

157

away. Out-of-doors, it is usually possible to protect TV and similar leads with thin piping.

Where to Watch Squirrels

Despite these unlovable aspects of the squirrel's persona in both country and town, the grey and red squirrel can provide hours of pleasure for the dedicated squirrel-watcher. Many people find the idea attractive but are at a loss to know when and where to look for them, how to know they are there, and how to watch them successfully.

Although one can observe squirrels at any time of the year—they are even about on cold winter days—it is better for one's morale to begin squirrel-watching when they are most plentiful or most active. In Chapter 6 we saw that maximum activity is associated with the summer months, next come spring and autumn, and lastly winter. Within any one season, the meteorological conditions have much bearing on whether or not one stands a good chance of seeing the

Female red squirrel on the bird table (B. S. Turner)

creatures. Heavy rain, overcast skies and strong winds are great discouragers of squirrel (and human) activity, and there is a better chance of seeing our furry friends on a bright, dry, snow-covered winter's day than if it is pouring with rain in the middle of July. But as summer is (theoretically) the sunniest season, May to August are prime squirrel-watching months.

There is a further advantage: from June to early August is the squirrel summer-breeding season, the time when the squirrels are least affected by the presence of humans. I have been not more than 8 metres (25ft) from a mating chase with no reaction from the squirrels whatever. Three days after this occasion, I turned round to change the film in my camera and found two squirrels copulating only 3·5 metres (12ft) from me. Time of day is also important. We know from Thompson's work (Chapter 6) that the squirrel's activity peak during any one day changes with the seasons. It is a very good idea to search for squirrels at midday during the winter, but in July—when the squirrel rests to avoid the noonday heat—such an expedition would be ill-timed.

The problem of where to watch squirrels is easily overcome. Hand-tame squirrels, such as our friend Nutkin, make observation easy, but although Nutkin may be delightful to watch, it must always be remembered that she is semi-domesticated so that, as far as wild behaviour is concerned, her actions must be suspect. They will almost certainly be affected by the proximity of humans and her desire to obtain food from them. For those who wish to observe squirrels *au naturel*, but near to home, other likely watching places must be sought.

One way is to use a hide, and attract the animals to it with a food bait. The hide does not have to be one of the elaborate camouflaged tents seen on wildlife programmes; any structure that masks the observer from the observed will work perfectly. A garden shed, a hedge, the conservatory at the back of the house, all can serve the purpose admirably. Once you have chosen a site for the hide, do not make the mistake of laying out your bait in a heap. If you do, then, as far as natural behaviour is concerned, you might just as well have stayed with a hand-tame squirrel. In the wild the squirrel's food is very thoroughly strewn about its habitat, a nut here, a toadstool there, and rarely if ever does the creature find an edible morsel without first having to forage in the undergrowth. Because of this squirrels very rarely fight over food: it comes in such small packages that as soon as it's found it's eaten, and there simply isn't time to pick a quarrel. But all this can change if the animals are artificially fed with maize or wheat left in a heap. Then there will be aggressive encounters and the strongest animal will sit atop the food pile and prevent others from feeding. In that sort of situation there will be very little chance of observing squirrel behaviour in the natural state—unless you are interested in the squirrel's fighting techniques! It is far better to scatter the seed far and wide over an area of 7 to 9 sq m (75 to 100 sq ft); that way every animal gets its fair share and there will be no ugly scenes.

Another excellent place to watch squirrels is your local park. Many now possess grey-squirrel populations, sometimes to the great chagrin of the park-keepers, many of whom regard the species as a pest. Parks are probably the best place for a town-bound naturalist to observe animals. Having lots more open space to move about in, the squirrels

In city park ?

are much less wary of humans. They get used to seeing people approaching or watching them, and become very blasé as a result, going about their business in a natural way with hardly a thought for their two-legged spectators. Thompson (1977) used this method in the USA, watching mating and other social interactions in a cemetery at Wisconsin.

In London, many of the gardens and parks have their quota of greys, but in my experience by far the best squirrel-watching ground is Holland Park, W.11. Here, much of the ground is fenced off from the public and given over to grass and rough natural growth. The grey squirrel obviously finds this agreeable and seems to act in a totally natural way. I have observed almost every kind of behaviour in this park: feeding, burying, antagonistic encounters, drey building, social grooming, solitary and social play, mating chases and the rearing of young.

To watch red squirrels one must travel further afield, away from the civilised surroundings of suburbia or urban parks into the wilderness areas of the British Isles. But this does not mean the west coast of Scotland or the mountains of Wales; red squirrels still exist in small pockets in the south of England, while in the north, the native species still holds its own in Cumbria, Northumberland and County Durham. There is even a possibility that the red squirrel is increasing in these regions. We recently observed red squirrels in a wood at Tow Law near our cottage in County Durham, and three days after this watched a single *S. vulgaris* crossing the road into a stand of pines only three miles from our home. Local enquiries proved red squirrels had not been seen in that locality for many years past.

One of the best locations for red-squirrel hunting is Forestry Commission land under pine trees, especially Scots pine (*Pinus sylvestris*). Normally, one must ask permission to enter these woods, but this is freely given if you can show that your request is a serious one. While you are in the forester's office, it is a good idea to ask which is the best areas for squirrels. A forester will know his section of the woods as well as his own back garden, and his help can be invaluable in locating a good study site. If no such help is available, choose mature Scots pine of 35 to 80 years of age—9 to 15m (30 to 50ft) tall. Between these ages the trees produce their maximum cone crop, and it will be here that red squirrels will almost certainly feed and make their dreys.

Finding Squirrel Signs

Once inside your study area the next task, unless you are using a hide to attract them, is to locate the squirrels. This is not as difficult as it sounds. It is true that squirrels are almost invisible in the trees, but if you know what to look and listen for, it is surprising how quickly you can run down your quarry.

The most obvious evidence that squirrels are in occupation of your study site will be feeding signs. These are scattered about the forest floor and anyone with a good eye should have no trouble in detecting them. Unfortunately, the feeding signs of red and grey squirrels are so similar that it is often impossible to distinguish between them with any degree of certainty. So be careful if both species are known to be present in your area. Where the squirrel is feeding throughout the year on pine seeds (an almost exclusively red-squirrel habit), the most obvious feeding signs will be the stripped central portions of the pine

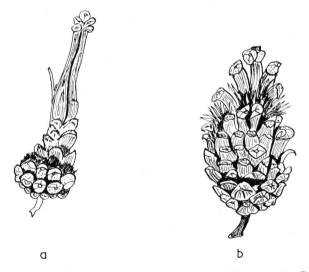

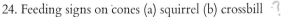

a   b

24. Feeding signs on cones (a) squirrel (b) crossbill

cone (the core). This is usually left with either a broad or narrow end (fig. 24), the central stem of the core being almost bare of pine scales except for their cut bases. Sometimes a few scales are left untouched at the apex of the cone. These cores are very characteristic of squirrel-feeding; the only creatures to produce a similar effect are cross-bills and woodpeckers, but their work is easily distinguished as the birds leave the cone intact and fray the scales in their attempts to extract the seed. Crossbills tend to splay the scales outwards, usually splitting them in the process, while woodpeckers twist and tear the scales producing a more ragged outline.

Between January and June, other signs may be on the forest floor: bitten-through pine shoots, bud-scales in compact groups, leaf buds with hollow centres. The position of these signs can be used to tell whether the animals were feeding in the canopy or on the ground. If most feeding is taking place in the trees, the cones, leaf buds etc. will be well scattered over the forest floor. Closely clumped cones indicate ground feeding, as the squirrel often takes its spoils to a favourite eating spot such as a tree stump.

Other signs of squirrel presence are continuous strips of bud-scales rolled back exposing the buds themselves, chewed flower buds, and fungal fruiting bodies (toadstools) with the distinctive marks of the squirrel's incisor teeth. Mice and voles also bite into toadstools, but their tooth impressions are much smaller than either the grey or the red squirrel's. During autumn and winter, in broad-leaved forests, the shells of nuts and acorns are good indicators of the presence of squirrels. Again, the problem is to distinguish which animal has been feeding— squirrel, mouse or even bird. Fortunately, most species leave tell-tale signs, as Gilbert White described over 100 years ago. The squirrel 'after rasping off the small end, splits the shell in two with his long foreteeth, as a man does with his knife' while the field-mouse 'nibbles a hole with her teeth, so regular as if drilled with a whimble, and yet so small that one would wonder how the kernel can be extracted through it'. The nuthatch, after securing the nut in some crevice 'picks an irregular hole with its bill'. Squirrel droppings are of little use to the squirrel spotter. Not only are they widely scattered and therefore extremely difficult to locate, they also vary in colour and shape depending on the diet of the squirrel at any particular time of the year.

Some clues are present the year round. If one examines the trunks of trees carefully it is often possible to discover characteristic scratch-marks on the bark, where the squirrel has climbed into the canopy. These take the form of three parallel lines made by the three longest digits of the fore or hind limb. Red squirrels also possess 'scratch points': in an area of deciduous trees in Thetford Chase, my wife pointed out a red squirrel. The little creature was standing upright at the base of the tree, hind-feet on the ground and scratching madly at an area of bark approximately 1·5m (5ft) and 300mm (1ft) wide. The action continued for around sixty seconds after which the squirrel made off across the ground. Grey squirrels are known to have definite marking points on trees and tree roots (see page 75). The grey-squirrel marking sites are often obvious from some distance, the bare patches of the tree showing up clearly against the dark grey/brown of the bark. Roe, red and fallow deer also make bark-free patches on trees, notably during the 'rut', or mating season when the male deer engages in threshing a hapless sapling with his horns, or when the bark's abrasive qualities are used in 'fraying' (removing) the skin or 'velvet' from the newly-formed antlers. Fortunately, one can distinguish between deer and squirrel sites in several ways. The squirrel marking-points are almost invariably made either at the base of the tree on a prominent root, or on the underside of its lowest branches. An older tree with a thickish trunk is usually chosen and, although there are seasonal differences, the sites are in use throughout the year. Deer usually fray on the vertical sections of a small tree or bush at the most convenient height for head-strikes with their antlers. Deer marking-sites are therefore usually 600mm to 1·8m (2-6ft) above ground and, unlike the squirrel, on sturdy saplings which 'give' when struck. When close to a marking site it is often possible to make out the claw and incisor marks of the squirrel, or the indentations where the 'tines' of deer's antlers have struck deeply into the wood.

On squirrel sites wet patches of urine may be visible (indicating very recent use) together with the odour of urine, faeces or glandular secretions. With deer sites urine and faeces will not be present, although male deer do use scent from facial glands to mark their

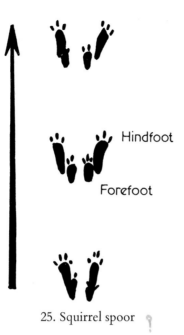

Hindfoot

Forefoot

25. Squirrel spoor

territory and generally scrape the earth around the fraying stock. Unbroken cobwebs over any site indicates that the animals have either left the area, or are concentrating their attentions elsewhere.

If the weather is wet or wintry, it may be possible to make out the spoor of the red or grey squirrel in mud or snow (fig 25). The tracks of the hind-feet are the most characteristic, as they often partly or completely obliterate the smaller imprints left by the forefeet. In the grey squirrel the hind-foot looks rather like a human hand, with the first toe on the inside of the foot occupying the same position as a thumb. On the forefoot there are four toes set around an almost rectangular pad, the claws usually showing distinctly. The track of the red squirrel is similar, but the pads are more delicate and there is less chance of the whole foot showing. The trail of both species is similar, the normal gait being a series of hops approximately a metre (3ft) in length. The tail is held high so that the scuff marks do not normally show. It is important not to confuse squirrel tracks with those of the rabbit. In the latter, the forefeet are often placed so close together that they leave only a single depression in mud or snow; this seldom happens with the squirrel. The squirrel's spoor is typified by longer claw marks and the whole imprint is much smaller and more delicate than the rabbit's.

Individual squirrels can often be located by sound. When feeding in the canopy, the red squirrel can be heard cracking cones some distance from its location. Sometimes a 'rain' of scales betrays the animal's presence. Squirrel calls are also useful locators; of its many calls, the alarm chatter is the easiest to hear and the most common. Once heard, it cannot be mistaken for that of any other animal. I first heard this call when watching greys—one moment the woods were full of them, the next they had vanished, while the canopy above and around me reverberated with the sound of chattering. At first I could not understand the reason for their alarm, but looking more closely at a patch of tall grass, I made out two black triangular objects peeping from above the waving stems, the ears of a feral cat. The cat stayed positioned for more than half an hour, during which time the squirrels' chattering hardly diminished. Since then, the sound has been imprinted in my brain.

Once the squirrel has been located, the observer's troubles have only just begun. It is possible to watch a tree squirrel fairly easily, and with binoculars (preferably 7 x 35) one can discern a useful amount of interesting behaviour. Feeding, locomotion, vocalisation and some aspects of social behaviour, are all amenable to this form of study. Unfortunately tree trunks, branches and leaves often obscure your 'target' at a vital moment, making such observation extremely frustrating. Alternatively, the beast will use the tree's long branches to cross to a second tree crown, leaving you to make your way through a giant growth of stinging nettles to your next point of vantage! After a while, the non-stop upward craning of the neck can induce quite painful spasms in and around the shoulders so that eventually you simply do not give a damn if you do miss a most unique piece of squirrel behaviour as long as you can hold your head in a less agonising position.

A squirrel on the ground is an altogether happier proposition from the watcher's point of view, although not from its own. A squirrel without its tree is like a soldier without a foxhole—in an extremely exposed position and in consequence, very wary indeed of the possibility of attack. So although a squirrel on the ground is much more comfortable to watch, it needs a considerable amount of woodmanship to get close enough to actually do any observation.

There are, of course, exceptions to this rule: my wife once followed a red squirrel and found it curled up asleep in the only bare patch of ground warmed by the spring sunshine; but generally some form of subterfuge is needed to get close enough to the wary sciurid. As with the suburban squirrel, a hide is probably the most useful way of studying the wild squirrel on the forest floor. Failing that it is a question of try, try and try again until one has sufficient expertise to stalk the squirrel successfully.

Photographing Squirrels

Once you are hooked on squirrel watching, you may want a permanent record of your observations. There are several ways of doing this: you can record your own observations on a tape cassette or tape squirrel vocalisations the same way, but most people prefer to record visually using a camera. For this you will need to be fairly well equipped—an instamatic may be fine for seaside snaps, but unless you are very, very lucky any squirrel shots you take will come out as no more than shapeless red or grey blobs. At very least, a single-lens reflex camera is required, perferably a large-format (6 x 6) camera, although the so-called miniature SLRs are now so good that these less expensive models will usually do just as well. For behavioural shots, additional equipment will be needed, a long-focus lens being the most important. As most of the observation on tree-living squirrels is done from a distance using binoculars, the telephoto must be quite powerful: 300mm lenses are barely adequate for this sort of work, a 600mm lens is probably better. There are two types of long-focus lens available: the usual telephoto which is quite bulky and heavy, and the mirror lens where a series of mirrors replaces most of the usual glass components. Mirror telephoto lenses are preferable; although bulky, they are light and not overly long, which helps in steadying the camera and ensures a clearer image on the negative. These lenses are not cheap and, worse still, even good lenses of this focal length leave a lot to be desired as regards image quality. However, if you go in for this sort of work, a pin-sharp photograph will (or should) concern you less than what the squirrel is actually doing.

When using long lenses it is almost impossible to hand-hold the camera-lens assembly; even with all this expensive equipment, your shots will come out looking as if they were taken by an instamatic unless you support the camera in some way. You can use a tripod, or even the branch of a tree, but by far the best means of steadying the equipment is a rifle grip which resembles the handle and stock of a machine gun, and serves the same purpose. Mounted on the rifle grip, the camera can be levelled much more easily, just as a rifle or machine gun is much more accurate than a hand-held revolver. The 'Novoflex' follow-focus system is probably the ultimate in this field; here you focus by squeezing a spring-loaded pistol grip instead of rotating the lens barrel.

For clearer photographs of natural behaviour, a hide once again comes into its own. The superb shots of red squirrels taken by Brian S. Turner (on pages 56, 59 and 158) were obtained using this technique— plus an almost superhuman amount of patience. Mr Turner explains his technique:

> To lure the squirrel into a position near the hide . . . we baited a suitably photogenic log with hazelnuts and acorns. It was placed on a drystone dyke, part of the squirrel's usual route to the nut trees, and by putting out the food only at certain times we gradually conditioned him to come during the short periods when the autumn sunlight shone.
>
> (Turner, 1978)

Before suitable photographs had been taken, even before the squirrel arrived, the nuts began to disappear. The mystery was solved when a short-tailed field vole was observed robbing the bait site, so the log was removed from the wall and set on smooth metal legs which were no problem for an agile squirrel but would present an insurmoutable barrier to mice and voles. Because the log was still very close to the drystone wall, this new site was soon discovered by the squirrel, and the feeding routine again established. Although thoroughly afraid of man, the squirrel soon became accustomed to the presence of the hide, and neither camera noise nor the rather awkward business of changing lenses seemed to interrupt him at his meal.

Mr Turner avoided the use of flash during his photographic sessions, for fear of frightening his subject. However, flash is a very useful tool; by greatly increasing the depth of field, more of the subject is brought into sharp focus. If you are able to set up flash-guns indoors for squirrel photography, so much the better. Purists will frown at this, but a tame squirrel is truly by far the best subject for portraiture. Not only can you control the subject to a far greater degree than in the wild, but lighting and 'props' can be manipulated until just the correct 'mix' has been obtained. It must be said, however, that such shots, while technically superb, somehow lack the true spirit or 'feel' of the infinitely more difficult wild-shot photographs.

Squirrels are not Good Pets!

And of course, you have first to find a tame squirrel. I do not recommend trying to tame a squirrel yourself. Squirrel infants found injured or at the mercy of wild animals are sometimes brought up in the human home, but this is the only time such hand-rearing is acceptable. It is illegal to keep grey squirrels, young or adult, in captivity (see page 38) and, given the present sorry state of the red squirrel in Britain, nest-robbing and hand-rearing of *S. vulgaris* for pleasure or photography is morally indefensible.

In any case, squirrels do not make very good pets. The old practice of keeping them in small cages with a single exercise-wheel has happily died out, although wheel and cage are perhaps no more cruel than any other sort of captivity. Unless the captive squirrel is allowed a tremendous amount of exercise, its claws can grow so long that it can hardly climb or move about. Squirrels can be kept in the comparative freedom of a house but, while not too bad a prison for the animal, its presence may become more than a little tiresome for the householder. M. H. Crawford (1959) has described the way in which pet squirrels:

will build a nest in some comfortable corner, making themselves at home and providing endless entertainment by their quaint ways. But to their quality of quaintness must be added another, less attractive one—that of destructiveness. Of course, they treat a civilised house as they would their native woods. They make their nests in places where they would not be disturbed . . . bookcases, couches and heavy screens that will not be moved for a few days . . . They also nibble cushions and chair legs. On the whole . . . they might be apt, in the end, to tire out the patience of their hosts.

Shorten (1954) relates how one of her female grey squirrels built a drey inside her piano! It is probably wise not to keep squirrels of any species in captivity unless one is completely devoted to them. It is almost impossible to give them sufficient exercise space, and they need so much watching that almost all one's waking hours would be spent preventing them getting into trouble. More important is the ethical question of whether we should derive pleasure or gratify our curiosity by keeping a wild animal in unnatural surroundings. Surely it is better to watch any creature in the freedom of its natural habitat. But to be certain that future generations will still have wild squirrel to watch, the controllers and planners of our forests will have to follow a few simple rules of conservation.

13
Conservation

Over the past 1,500 years or so the British Isles have lost a great deal of their native fauna, including the beaver, wild boar, bear and wolf. We even had a huge wild ox, the aurochs, *Bos primigenius*, perhaps the most impressive of these vanished species. The aurochs was truly a massive beast, with huge curved horns sometimes over 1m (3ft) in length and not unlike those of the modern-day Wild White Cattle of England. It stood more than 2m (7ft) high at the shoulder and must have towered awesomely above the average 1·5m (5ft) hunter of the Neolithic. Yet it was these same hunters, or their descendants, who put paid to all these beautiful creatures: with the aurochs it was deforestation and hunting; with the beaver it was fur trapping, and with the wolf a mixture of hunting and pure bigotry. So we should seriously consider the possibility that some of our remaining species might die out within the next few decades because of man's stupidity or lack of foresight.

Today the United Kingdom is becoming more and more urbanised —picturesque villages are ringed with motorways, and unsightly conurbations spread like a cancer along the main arterial roads. Those people charged with the responsibility for our environment, the planners of city and county hall, are either unwilling or unable to stop the seemingly mindless 'progress'. They have become fettered with the chains of their own expertise; having learned in college that to speed up car-flow through urban areas was a 'good thing' they continue to apply this maxim, even when the cost of increased vehicle through-put is anonymous clearways and soulless pedestrian underpasses, covered with obscene graffiti and stinking of urine or worse. Children grow up in an almost completely azooic environment, knowing at

171

most the names of sparrow and starling, and then we wonder why they rebel! Trees are planted in the suburbs, but only in 'pretty' ones and twos, giving no heed to the requirements of birds, bats or squirrels who might make their home in them if planted in a more natural way. Simultaneously with such puerile tree planting, whole areas of coniferous forest—perfect red-squirrel habitat—are drowned to make reservoirs to feed our giant petrochemical industries, half of which produce commodities superfluous to our needs. The British red squirrel, a unique subspecies, is already in decline—what are its chances of surviving into the twenty-first century?

As far as danger from the grey squirrel is concerned, the chances are very good indeed. True, the grey has occupied much of the red squirrel's former range, but for the present at least it is unable to occupy those areas which are now red-squirrel strongholds—the coniferous forests, either natural or planted. Here, the red should be relatively safe from its larger, more aggressive cousin. Only if the introduced species begins colonisation of such areas will the red squirrel be in serious danger from it. But *S. carolinensis* will not enter large stands of conifers and therefore, at present, the grey squirrel is no threat to the survival of the native *S. vulgaris*.

The crucial factor for the red squirrel is man's attitude to the management and structure of his forests. Swift and thoughtful action is needed to be certain of the red squirrel's survival: we can either decide to grow our timber in the traditional way—by raising stands of similarly aged trees and then clear-felling when they have reached the target age; or we can mix and modify forestry procedure so that the red squirrel suffers the minimum of disturbance. It is also possible to devise a forest-management plan that would actually encourage red-squirrel colonisation of woodland and, once established, help the population to maintain itself at a high level.

In the short term we can help the red squirrel (being such a pest the grey should in no way be encouraged) by stepping in with food and other services during especially severe weather. Where an area is susceptible to drought, standing water should be provided. Most plantations have water tanks at strategic intervals along the forest rides to help contain forest fires; it should be possible to modify such tanks so that red squirrel (and other animals) can drink without the danger of falling into these often steep-sided receptacles and drowning. Roofs on the many forest huts could serve as catchment areas for a small trough, thereby providing water without the need for periodic refilling (Tittensor, 1975).

In certain years the red squirrels' stable source of food may fail completely, and if no help is forthcoming, they may suffer considerable mortality (Nixon and McClain, 1969). During such times, artificial foodstuffs should be used to supplement the squirrels' natural diet and to tide them over the lean months. This need not be as expensive as it sounds; wheat grains or whole maize are relatively cheap, and it is surprising how little would have to be deployed in order to save a substantial proportion of the red-squirrel population.

Where neither food nor cover limit the species' population, it may be possible to increase red-squirrel numbers by installing nest boxes in suitable positions on nest-trees. Nest-boxes can help to double a population where lack of nesting sites is a limiting factor (Burger, 1969), but, in areas where grey-squirrel invasion is known to be a

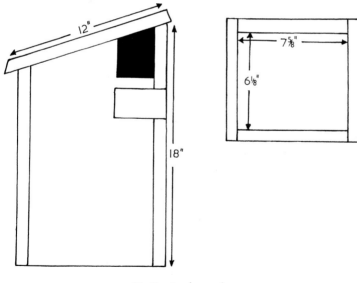

26. Squirrel nest-box

173

possibility, special precautions must be observed. Nest-boxes in these areas must not be attractive to both native and introduced species, as the grey squirrel will almost certainly always 'win' if the two squirrels compete for nesting space. Luckily, the grey squirrel is larger and heavier than the red, and will therefore require a larger entrance hole to gain admittance to any nest-box. Yoakuin and Dasmaun (1969) state that a hole 63mm (2½in) in diameter is just wide enough to allow a grey squirrel to enter, so if the hole is made smaller than this (say, 51mm (2in) diameter) the grey squirrel will find it very difficult to gain entrance to the nest-box while the hole should prove no trouble to the smaller red. While studying the St. Vincent parrot (*Amazona guildingii*) in the Caribbean, I learned that the Puerto Rican parrot (*A.vittata*), a species on the verge of extinction, had suffered from a lack of nesting space. The problem had been neatly solved by drilling nest-holes into living trees with a heavy-duty augur, and the numbers of *A.vittata* had risen so considerably that the species was no longer in grave danger of extirpation. This solution could be used to provide nesting sites for *S. vulgaris*.

All the above suggestions are, unfortunately, stop-gap measures; they will help in the short term but looking further ahead other solutions must be found. The crux of the whole problem lies in the structure of the forests themselves. Given suitable coniferous habitat, the red squirrel can take care of itself in the short-term. What is needed is a well-managed and ecologically sound long-term forestry plan. Dr Andrew Tittensor is perhaps the only scientist in the British Isles who has studied this problem in depth over a period of years. His management recommendations form the basis of the eight-point plan below:

1   As the red squirrel's primary (and safest) habitat in Great Britain is Scots-pine forest, conservation of the species should concentrate heavily upon this type of habitat.
2   Squirrel-orientated habitat should consist of a large continuous acreage of conifer woodland, preferably not less than 100 hectares and where possible, over 1,000 hectares in extent. A high proportion of the trees should be Scots pine, but additional conifer species scattered

throughout the woodland are advantageous. These latter would be invaluable secondary food sources should the Scots pine suffer cone-crop failure.

3   It is essential that a large proportion of the trees should be of cone-bearing age. Scots pine generally bears cones between approximately 15 and 100 years of age, with the best crops between 35 and 80 years. Throughout this period the tree produces cones fairly reliably. After a full century of life, cone production declines and the tree becomes overmature. Scots pines of 35 to 80 years therefore provide a steady food supply, as well as maximum cover and nesting sites.

4   The best way to provide such trees over a long period is by planting a continuous succession of different ages. These should be thinned at intervals to allow development of a full canopy layer, facilitating squirrel movement via aerial highways. Overmature trees should be thinned gradually, rather than clear-felled at a stroke.

5   In certain areas the squirrel population may grow so high that they may damage their own habitat and, because of their high density, become vulnerable to epidemic disease. Culling of a segment of the

Grey at the garden fence

population should be carried out in these circumstances. Alternatively, the excess population may be trapped and moved elsewhere (see 6 below).

6 Where conifer plantations are grown in areas where there is no remaining red-squirrel population to act as a breeding nucleus, reintroduction of captured squirrels from other areas can be attempted. Because of the possibility of damage to trees, it is as well to consult the local Forestry Commission Office before beginning such a course of action.

7 We do not yet know how human activity affects the red squirrel, but there is no doubt that red squirrels seem less able than the grey to withstand prolonged contact with man, and the noisy environment that usually surrounds him. Human interference should, therefore, be held to minimum levels in forest plantations or stopped entirely in selected areas.

8 Secondary food sources, such as seed-bearing mast and seed-bearing deciduous trees and shrubs should be provided, scattered in small groups throughout the woodland.

Point 8 raises one large problem. As soon as broad-leaved deciduous trees form a part of the plantation, the area at once becomes more attractive to the grey squirrel, and the greater is the possibility that it will make a permanent appearance. If the area is liable to grey-squirrel invasion, special precautions must be taken to keep down the broad-leaved content of the woodland. As we do not know at just what percentage of broad-leaved trees an area becomes able to support grey squirrels, it is as well to err on the side of caution. Tittensor (1975) believes the critical minimum level to be below 25 per cent, and it is probably much lower. Provided such considerations are borne in mind, it should be possible to fulfil the stipulations of point 8, giving the red squirrel a secondary food supply but at the same time making the area just not attractive enough to encourage grey-squirrel settlement.

The management proposals outlined above are offered in the hope that all interested forest managers will apply at least some of these realistic and relatively inexpensive suggestions. The ordinary person can help by asking whether such plans are being implemented whenever he visits a recreational area in one of the nation's Forest Parks. Despite the modern creed of maximising output and optimising profits, we still have an obligation to the natural world which our technology has damaged so badly. Were this Eight Point Plan to be implemented, we could be quite sure that the red squirrel, the prettiest of our woodland fauna, would not only beat the threat of foreign competition, but would also be around to delight our children and our children's children well into the twenty-first century.

Appendices

1 GREY-SQUIRREL INTRODUCTIONS FROM 1902

Area Released	Date	Number	Origin
Kingston Hill, Richmond, London	1902	100	USA?
Wrexham, Denbighshire	1903	5	Woburn
Lyme, Cheshire	1903–4	25	?
Regent's Park, London	1905–7	91	Woburn
Malton, North Yorkshire	1906	36	Woburn
Kew Gardens, London	1908	4	Woburn
Farnham Royal, Buckinghamshire	1908	?	USA
Farnham Royal, Buckinghamshire	1909	5	USA
Frimley, Surrey	1910	8	USA
Dunham, Cheshire	1910	2	?
Sandling, Kent	1910	?	?
Bramhall, Cheshire	1911–12	5	Woburn
Birmingham, Warwickshire	1912	?	?
Bedale, North Yorkshire	1913	?	?
Bingley, West Yorkshire	1914	14	London
Darlington, Co. Durham	1914–15	?	?
Exeter, Devon	1915	4	?
Stanwick, Northamptonshire	1918	2	?
Dunfermline, Scotland	1919	?	?
Bournemouth, Hampshire	?	6	London
Hebden Bridge, West Yorkshire	1921	8	?
Aberdare, Mid Glamorgan	1922	?	London
Needwood Forest, Staffordshire	1929	2	Bournemouth

2 RED-SQUIRREL FOOD IN BRITAIN

		Authority						
		a	b	c	d	e	f	g
Trees	Nuts, berries, winged seeds (especially conifers)	×	×	×	×	×	×	×
	Pollen					×	×	
	Leaf and flower buds	×		×	×	×	×	×
	Young, leafy shoots	×	×	×	×	×	×	×
	Inner bark and sap	×	×	×	×	×	×	
Shrubs	Nuts and berries	×	×	×	×	×	×	×
	Pollen					×		×
Herbs	Berries and seeds (many types)	×	×	×	×	×	×	
	Pollen and stamens of flowers		×		×	×		
	Green leaves			×	×			×
	Roots			×	×			
	Bulbs and tubers		×	×	×	×		
Domestic	Agricultural grain			×				×
	Garden and orchard fruits	×	×	×	×	×		×
Fungi	Large fruiting bodies	×	×	×	×	×	×	×
	Hyphae under bark			×				
Insects	Eggs, larvae, pupae and adults			×	×	×		
Birds	Eggs, young and small adults	×	×	×	×	×		
Others	Soil				×			
	Bones and antlers			×	×			
	Bark and wood					×	×	×
	Exotic nuts (brazil, coconut, etc.)*	×						×
	Maize and small grain			×		×	×	×
	Biscuit and dog biscuit*					×		×
	Oily seeds (sunflower)*					×		×
	Caraway seed*	×	×					
	Greenstuff (lettuce, cabbage, etc.)*							×

* Captive animals.

a Harvie-Brown, 1880–1
b Millais, 1905
c Barrett-Hamilton and Hinton, 1921
d Shorten 1954, 1957*a*
e Shorten, 1962 *a, b*
f Tittensor (field), 1970
g Tittensor (captive), 1970

3 DREY DIMENSIONS

Drey number	Total weight (gm)	Twig-frame weight (gm)	Lining weight (gm)	Mean external diameter (cm)
1	638	367	271	35
2	302	190	112	28
3	198	80	118	28
4	287	141	146	26
5	215	66	149	27
6	283	143	140	27
7	253	200	53	30
8	195	76	119	24
9	209	79	130	25
10	273	130	143	24
11	269	133	136	25
12	463	307	156	30
Mean	298.7	159.3	139.4	27.4

(Source: Tittensor, 1970*b*)

4 GREY-SQUIRREL SIGNALS

Visual Signals

Signal	Context	Probable Function
Gentle flicks of tail	Following fright or surprise	To elicit recognisable response from cause (may include second squirrel of unknown disposition)
Rapid tail-flapping over back dorso-ventrally	While running or dashing away	Warning signal of approach of predator
Slow raising of tail over back	While sitting; on approach of squirrel	Response to approaching animal
Rapid tail-flapping	In presence of another squirrel	Strongly agonistic; intimidation
Expansion of tail hair	In presence of another squirrel	Intimidation; indication of dominance

Signal	Context	Probable Function
Relaxation of tail hair	In presence of another squirrel	Appeasement; indication of subordination
Ears moved forward showing white fur	Encounter between squirrels	Intimidation; indication of dominance
Ears moved back covering white fur	Encounter between squirrels	Appeasement; indication of subordination
Eyelids partially closed, eye narrowed	Encounter between squirrels	Intimidation; indication of dominance
Eyelids wide open, eye rounded	Encounter between squirrels	Appeasement; indication of subordination
Repeated dilation of nostrils	Encounter between squirrels	Indication of olfactory testing?
Using teeth to tear bark or wood	Encounter between squirrels, or at marking point	Intimidation; indication of dominance
Teeth used in ritual gnawing or feeding	Stressful conditions	Release of stress, particularly when near other squirrels
Alternate paddling motion with hind-feet	Encounter between squirrels	Intention movement; attempt to secure dominance
High, alert standing on hind-legs showing white ventral fur	Another squirrel or predator seen	Indication of predator or strange squirrel
Flashing white fur on front of breast	Hopping progression	Indication of presence and whereabouts of squirrel
Size of testes and colour vary with state of development	Exhibited when in sitting up posture	Indication to other squirrels of sexual condition
Erection of mid-dorsal body hair	Highly aggressive encounter	Intimidation

181

Signal	Context	Probable Function
Running at	Another squirrel	Indication of domiance and to remove the presence of the other squirrel
Lolloping trot	Male searching for female on heat	Advertises the presence, in strange territory, of this animal
Walk high on all four legs	Male approach to female	Indication of intent to 'test' female
Creeping progression	In presence of another squirrel	Indicates no intention of attack; subservience
Deliberate walk	At another squirrel	Indication that the other squirrel should move

Auditory Signals

Signal	Context	Probable Function
Teeth-chatter	Encounter between squirrels	Intimidation; indication of dominance
Mouth-smacking	In close presence of another squirrel	Indication of discomfort of situation?
Gnawing sound	In presence of another squirrel	Intimidation
Low intensity 'tuk . . . tuk . . . tuk'	Juvenile in presence of mother	Recognition; soliciting call
Purring sound, repetitive	Male, while foot-stamping by female	Appeasement prior to 'testing'
Purring, only slight repetition; 'prr . . .prr'	Two familiar squirrels placed together	Recognition
A snorting call, 'chuff . . .chuff'	Males searching for lost female on heat	Indicates presence of female on heat and as aid to her relocation

Signal	Context	Probable Function
Single snort	Predator seen when young are about	Warning to young and other squirrels
'chuck-chuck-chuck-chareeee', changing to 'chareeee' alone and finally only 'eeeoooo', lasting perhaps 20 minutes	Response to cat, fox or (?) predator, or to other squirrels calling. Also by female on hole, or made by male near female on heat	Indication of whereabouts of predator; whereabouts of squirrel; female on heat
Piercing squeal	Fearful juvenile	Call for mother and attempt to secure release
Loud shriek	Fearful adult	Warning and attempt to secure release
Repeated squeaks	Squirrel chased closely by another	Appeasement; indication of subordination
Low-intensity trill or or squeak	Two squirrels close together in trap	Unknown, but not antagonistic
Rapid 'shuck-shuck-shuck'	Prior to hasty entry to hole, or made by male nearest female on heat	Warning of imminent entry into hole or nest
Growling, ranging from a quiet 'mm-mm' through an open-mouthed growl modulated by mouth movements to a loud 'squeecharr-charr' call	Done towards a second squirrel	Connected with defence and warding off other unwanted squirrels

Scent Signals

Signal	Context	Probable Function
Sweet nutty smell from dermal gland	Always present, may be accentuated by excitement	Individual recognition by other squirrels, possession of nest, used by males tracking females on heat

Signal	Context	Probable Function
Moderate tangy scent from urine	On marking points from males (breeding season), also along branches by both sexes	Individual recognition, indication of area occupation by squirrels and of visitation by other squirrels
Faeces produce strong sweetish scent	Faeces deposited on objects and anus wiped along branches Also on marking points during autumn	Not known, possibly as above

Physical Contact

Signal	Context	Probable Function
Lashing out with front feet, can cause lacerations	Exhibited towards another squirrel in defence situations	To avoid injury when flight impossible and to ward off another animal in an attempt to keep a desirable item
Bipedal eviscerating action with hind-feet	During direct attack in fighting	Defensive
Biting with incisors	Performed by dominant animal during chases	Indication of superiority
Jumping at	Performed by dominant animal only when on ground	Indication of superiority
Using mouth and forepaws in mutual grooming	Cohabiting squirrels inside or near nest	Bond maintenance
Sliding body over the top of another squirrel	Cohabiting squirrels	Bond maintenance
Homosexual behaviour between males	Usually in association with mating chase	Redirection of frustrated sexual drive

Bibliography

Abbott, R. J., Bevercombe, G. P. & Rayner, A. D. M. (1977) Sooty bark disease of sycamore and the grey squirrel. *Trans*, British Mycological Society. *69* (3), 507–508.

Allen, D. L. (1943) Michigan Fox Squirrel Management. Michigan.

Altum, B. (1873) Beschädigungen an Eichen durch Eichhörnchen. Z. Forest-u Jagdw. *5*, 87–88.

Andrews, C. W. (1900) *Zoology: Mammalia. A monograph of Christmas Island*. London.

Anthony, H. E. (1928) *Field Book of North American mammals*. New York.

Bakken, A. (1959) *Behaviour of the grey squirrel*. South East Association, Game & Fish Commissioners, *13*, 393–406.

Barkalow, F. S. & Soots, R. F. (1965) An analysis of the effect of artificial nest boxes on a grey squirrel population. *Trans*. N. American Wildlife Conference. *30*, 349–59.

Barrett-Hamilton, G. E. H. & Hinton, M. A. C. (1921) *A History of British Mammals*, 683–720. London.

Blackmore, D. K. & Owen, D. G. (1968) Ectoparasites: the significance in British wild rodents. *Symposia*, Zoological Society of London. *24*, 197–220.

Bourliere, F. (1956) *The Natural History of Mammals*. London.

Bozhko, S. I. (1975) On the breeding success of birds in Leningrad USSR parks. *Acta Biol*. Debrecina *12*, 57–60.

Brander, R. B. & Cochran, W. W. (1971) *Wildlife Management Techniques*. The Wildlife Society. Washington, D.C.

Burger, G. V. (1969) Response of grey squirrel to next boxes at Remington Farms, Maryland. *Journal of Wildlife Management*. *33*, 796–801.

Christian, J. J. (1963) Endocrine adaptive mechanisms & the physiologic regulation of population growth. In *Physiological Mammology*. Vol 1. New York.

Collier, E. (1957) Revolutionary new trap. *Outdoor Life*. Sept, 38–41.

Crawford, M. H. (1959) The red squirrel and its relatives. In *Britain's Wonderland of Nature*. London.

Davidson, W. R. (1976) Ectoparasites of selected populations of grey squirrel (*Sciurus carolinensis*) in the South-Eastern United States.

Donohoe, R. W. (1965) Squirrel harvest and population studies in Ohio. In *Game Research in Ohio*. Vol 3, pp 65–93. Columbus.

Douglas-Hamilton, I. & Douglas-Hamilton, O. (1979) *Among the Elephants*. London.

Eibl-Eibesfeldt, I. (1951) Beobachtungen zur Fortpflanzungsbiologie und Jugendent-wicklung des Eichhörnchens (*Sciurus vulgaris*, L.) *Zeitschrift Tierpsychologie. 8*, 370–400.

Eibl-Eibesfeldt, I. (1967) Concepts of ethology and their significance in the study of human behaviour. In *Early Behaviour*. London

Eibl-Eibesfeldt, I. (1970) *Ethology: the Biology of Behaviour*. New York.

Ellerman, J. R. & Morrison-Scott, T. C. S. (1951) Checklist of Palaearctic and Indian mammals 1758 to 1946. London.

Farrentinos, R. C. (1974) Social communication of the tassel-eared squirrel (*Sciurus aberti*): a descriptive analysis. *Zeitschrift Tierpsychologie. 34*(5), 441–458.

Ferron, J. (1975) Solitary play of the red squirrel (*Tamiasciurus hudsonicus*). *Canadian Journal of Zoology. 53*(11), 1495–1499.

Fitzwater, W. D. (1943) Colour marking of mammals with special reference to squirrel. *Journal of Wildlife Management. 7*, 190–192.

Formosof, A. N. (1933) The crop of cedar nuts, invasion into Europe of the Siberian Nutcracker (*Nucifraga caryocatactes macrorhynchus*, Brehm) and fluctuations in numbers of the squirrel (*Sciurus vulgaris*, L). *Journal of Animal Ecology. 2*, 70–81.

Frank, H. (1952) Über die Jugendentwicklung des Eichhörnchens. *Zeitschrift Tier-psychologie. 9*, 12–22.

Gewalt, W. (1975) Quoted in *Animal Life Encyclopaedia*. New York.

Goodall, J. (1971) *In The Shadow of Man*, London.

Hanson, E. V. & Weigl, P. D. (1975) Observational learning and the feeding ener-getics of the red squirrel (*Tamiasciurus hudsonicus*). *Americas' Zoology. 15*(3), 794.

Harvie-Brown, J. A. (1880/81) The squirrel in Great Britain. *Proc Royal Physical Society*. Edinb. *5*, 343–348; *6*, 31–63 & 115–183.

Hoglund, N. H. (1960) Studier över näringen vintertid hos marden *Martes m. martes* Linn. i Jamtlands län. Vildrevy, *1*, 319–337.

Horwich, R. H. (1972) The ontogeny of social behaviour in the grey squirrel (*Sciurus carolinensis*). Berlin.

Jones, J. C. (1961) Squirrel problems and what to do about them. *Pest Control. 29*(8), 14–22.

Kiris, I. D. (1941) Methods for forecasting changes in population of the common squirrel (*Sciurus vulgaris* L). In Russian. *Trans Central Laboratory Biology & Game Industry*. Moscow. *5*, 17–34.

Kjelsaas, D. (1972) Squirrel (*Sciurus vulgaris*) licks maple sap. *Fauna* (Oslo). *25*(2), 122.

Kurten, B. (1968) *Pleistocene Mammals of Europe*. London.

Laidler, K. (1978) *Language in the Orang-utan? In Action, Gesture and Symbol*. London.

Laidler, K. (1980) *The Talking Ape*. London.

Ljubimov, M. P. (1935) *Diseases of Squirrels*. In Russian. English summary in: The biology of the hare and the squirrel, and their diseases. Moscow.

Loizois, C. (1966) Play in mammals. *Symposia Zoological Society of London*. Vol 18.

Lorenz, K. (1969) *On Aggression*. London.

Luhring, R. (1928) Das Harkleid von *Sciurus vulgaris* L. und die Verteilung seiner Farbvarianten in Deutschland. *Zeitschrift für Morphologie der Tiere. 11*, 667–762.

Lundberg, G. (1946) Squirrel damage to spruce plantations. In Swedish. *Skogen, 33*, 204–205.

Metzger, C. (1946) On the squirrel as a pest of pine. In Swedish. *Skogen. 33*, 132.

Middleton, A. D. (1931). *The Grey Squirrel.* London.

Middleton, A. D. (1932) The grey squirrel (*Sciurus carolinensis*) in the British Isles, 1930–1932. *Journal of Animal Ecology. 1*, 166–167.

Millais, J. G. (1905) *The Mammals of Great Britain and Ireland.* Vol 2. London.

Moore, J. C. (1968) Sympatric species of tree squirrel mix in mating chase. *Journal of Mammology. 49*(3), 531–533.

Mortenson, P. H. (1965) The immigration of the red squirrel (*Sciurus vulgaris*) north of the Limfjord. In Danish, English summary. *Flora Fauna Silkebord. 71*, 73–79.

Naumov, N. P. (1934) Determining the age of the squirrel (*Sciurus vulgaris* L.). In Russian. *Uchen Zap Moscow University. 2*, 275–291.

Nixon, C. M., Beal, R. O. & Donohoe, R. W. (1968) Grey squirrel litter movement monitored by radio transmitter. *Journal of Mammalogy. 49*(3), 560.

Nixon, C. M. & McClain, M. W. (1969) Squirrel population decline following a late spring frost. *Journal of Wildlife Management. 33*(2), 353–357.

Ognev, S. I. (1940) *Mammals of the USSR and Adjacent Countries.* Vol 4, *Rodents,* translated from the Russian. Israel Programme for Scientific Translations, 1966.

Oxley, D. J., Fenton, M. M. & Carmody, G. R. (1974) The effects of roads on populations of small mammals. *Annals of Applied Ecology. 11*(1), 51–59.

Polyakov, I. J. (1959) Ground squirrel control in the USSR. Report Int Conf on Harmful Mammals and their Control. Eur & Medit Plant Protection Organisation. Paris.

Pudney, J. Seasonal changes in testis and epididymus of the American Grey Squirrel (*Sciurus carolinensis*). *Journal of Zoology.* London. *179*, 107–120.

Pullianen, E. (1963) Spiral bark-stripping (ring-barking) of the pine by the squirrel (*Sciurus vulgaris*). In Finnish, English summary. *Suomen Riista. 16*, 56–58.

Pullianen, E. & Salonen, K. (1963) On ring-barking of the pine squirrel (*Sciurus vulgaris*) in Finland. *Suomalainen Tiedeakat, Toim.* (*Sarja IV Biologica*). *72*, 1–29.

Ratcliffe, D. A. (1970) Changes attributable to pesticides in egg breakage frequency and eggshell thickness in some British birds. *Journal of Applied Ecology. 7*, 67–115.

Ratcliffe, D. A. (1972) The peregrine population of Great Britain in 1971. *Bird Study. 19*, 117–156.

Raspopov, M. P. & Isakov, S. A. (1935) On the Biology of the Squirrel. In Russian, English summary. In *The biology of the hare and the squirrel, and their diseases.* Moscow.

Rowe, J. J. (1973) Grey squirrel control. Forestry Commission leaflet No 56. London.

Sharp, W. M. (1959) A commentary on the behaviour of free-running grey squirrels. In *Symposium on the Grey Squirrel. Proc SE Association, Game & Fish Commission. 13*, 382–387.

Short, H. L. & Duke, W. B. (1971) Seasonal food consumption and body weights of captive tree squirrels. *Journal of Wildlife Management. 35*(3), 435–439.

Shorten, M. (1954) *Squirrels.* London.

Shorten, M. (1957) Damage caused by squirrels in Forestry Commission areas. 1954–56. *Forestry. 30*, 151–172.

Shorten, M. (1962a) Squirrels, their biology and control. Ministry of Agriculture, Fisheries & Food *Bulletin.* 184. London.

Shorten, M. (1962b) *Red Squirrels.* London.

Shorten, M. & Courtier, F. A. (1955) A population study of the grey squirrel (*Sciurus carolinensis*) in May, 1954. *Annals of Applied Biology. 43*, 494–510.

Smith, N. B. & Barkalow, F. S. Jnr. (1967) Precocious breeding in the grey squirrel. *Journal of Mammalogy. 48*(2), 328–330.

Spärck, R. (1936) Contribution to Danish zoogeography and faunistics. IV. On the distribution and abundance of red squirrels in Denmark. In Danish. *Vidensk Meddr dansk naturh Foren. 99*, 267–281.

Taylor, J. C. (1968) The use of marking points by grey squirrels. *Journal of Zoology. 155*, 146–147.

Taylor, J. C. (1975) An example of how variations in behaviour can invalidate population estimates. *Australian Mammalogy. 1*(4), 403–404.

Taylor, J. C. (1977) The frequency of grey squirrel (*Sciurus carolinensis*) communication by use of scent mark points. *Journal of Zoology.* London. *183*(4), 543–545.

Thomas, O. (1896). The seasonal changes in the common squirrel. *Zoologist, 20*, 401–407.

Thompson, D. C. (1977a) The social system of the grey squirrel. *Behaviour. 64*(3–4), 305–328.

Thompson, D. C. (1977b) Reproductive behaviour of the grey squirrel. *Canadian Journal of Zoology. 55*(7), 1176–1184.

Thompson, D. C. (1977c) Diurnal and seasonal activity of the grey squirrel (*Sciurus carolinensis*). *Canadian Journal of Zoology. 55*(7), 1185–1189.

Tittensor, A. M. (1970a) The ecology of the red squirrel (*Sciurus vulgaris*, L.) in relation to its food resource. PhD thesis, Edinburgh.

Tittensor, A. M. (1970b) Red squirrel dreys. *Journal of Zoology.* London. *162*, 528–533.

Tittensor, A. M. (1975) Red Squirrel. *Forestry Commission For Rec.* 101. London.

Turček, F. J. (1959) Zur Nährung des Eichhörnchens—*Sciurus vulgaris fuscoater* Altum 1876 in der Slowakei (CSR). *Waldygiene 3*, 50–53.

Turner, B. (1978) Pers, comm.

Uhlig, H. G. (1957) Grey squirrel populations in extensive forested areas of West Virginia. *Journal of Wildlife Management. 21*, 335–341.

Yoakum J. & Dasmann, W. P. (1969) Habitat manipulation practices. *Wildlife Management Techniques.* The Wildlife Society. Washington, DC.

Zawoiska, E. (1958) Geographical distribution of the dark phase of the squirrel (*Sciurus vulgaris fuscoater* Altum) in Poland. *Acta theriol. 2*, 159–174.

Index

190

tree barking, 118-22
tree squirrels, 7-8, 12, 13, 19; *see also*
    Sciurus carolinensis, Sciurus vulgaris
Turner, Brian S., 168-9

urination posture, 92

vibrassae *see* whiskers

Warfarin, 133-4
weasel, 111
whiskers, functions of, 25
White's squirrel *see Sciurus whitei*
wild cat, 67, 109, 110
Woburn Abbey, 37
woodchuck, 16
woodmouse *see Apodemus sylvatica*